Good, Bad, No Dad?

A Biblical Reflection on the Father Deficit in Contemporary Society

by John Woods

To Amol

Thanks for your voice on air.

"By the spirit we cry "Abba Father""

John

GRACE PUBLICATIONS TRUST
62 Bride Street
London N7 8AZ
www.gracepublications.co.uk

First published in Great Britain by Grace Publications Trust 2025.

© John Woods 2025

The right of John Woods to be identified as the author of this work has been asserted by him under the Copyright, Designs and Patents Act 1988. All rights reserved.

No part of this publication may be reproduced, stored in a retrieval system or transmitted in any form by any means, electronic, mechanical, photocopying, recording or otherwise, without the prior permission of the publisher or the Copyright Licensing Agency.

A record for this book is available from the British Library.

All Scripture quotations, unless otherwise indicated, are taken from the Holy Bible, New International Version®, NIV®. Copyright ©1973, 1978, 1984, 2011 by Biblica, Inc.™ Used by permission of Zondervan. All rights reserved worldwide. www.zondervan.com The "NIV" and "New International Version" are trademarks registered in the United States Patent and Trademark Office by Biblica, Inc.™

Cover design by Pete Barnsley (CreativeHoot.com)

Printed in the UK by Verite C M Ltd

ISBN Paperback: 978-1-912154-97-5
Ebook: 978-1-912154-98-2

Good, Bad, No Dad?

A Biblical Reflection on the Father Deficit in Contemporary Society

by John Woods

Grace Publications

To Oscar, Cosette, Cecily and Felicity, treasured grandchildren and their excellent dads, Tom and Ashley.

Contents

Foreword   7

Introduction   10

Chapter 1:   15
What is it to be fatherless?

Chapter 2:   30
Human fathers in the biblical story ~ Old Testament

Chapter 3 ~ Interviews: 54
Repairing the broken picture
~ Different backgrounds, same wounds

Chapter 4 ~ Case Study: 79
Judges 11 – 12 Jephthah

Chapter 5 ~ Interview: 91
Mending the broken hallelujah ~ Child abuse

Chapter 6:   111
God the Father in the biblical story ~ Old Testament

Chapter 7 ~ Interview: 125
Fatherless in Latvia ~ The influence of culture

Chapter 8:	*135*
Human fathers in the biblical story ~ New Testament	
Chapter 9 ~ Interviews:	*150*
Lost too Early	
Chapter 10:	*174*
God the Father in the biblical story ~ New Testament	
Chapter 11 ~ Interview:	*197*
Adopted	
Chapter 12:	*210*
Prayer that joins the dots ~ The Christian's response	
Chapter 13 ~ Testimony:	*221*
Turning to our Heavenly Father	
Conclusion:	*227*
Knowing our Heavenly Father	
Acknowledgements	*237*
Bibliography	*239*

Foreword

This is a book that I needed to read years ago. Like John, my father, more precisely my biological father, is 'unknown'. I was born in 1968 to a young schoolgirl who had got pregnant at the end of the summer holidays. I know little about her, but almost nothing about my father. He disappeared from the scene when she discovered she was pregnant. I don't know his name.

I was fortunate to be adopted into a caring family and to have an adoptive Dad. There was no abuse, and he worked hard and sacrificed to give me a great education and opportunities in life he had not enjoyed growing up in a working-class home. He was a child of the 1930s and was not emotionally open or close during my childhood. This was compounded by the fact that my parents had a difficult marriage, and I was, as the oldest son, closer to my mother. Sadly, my dad died of cancer when I was in my early twenties, just as we were beginning to connect at a more adult level. Like many sons I was discovering a greater closeness to my dad as an adult and greater understanding of what life had been like for him. Mark Twain was spot on when he wrote, with irony:

> When I was a boy of 14, my father was so ignorant I could hardly stand to have the old man around. But when I got to be 21, I was astonished at how much the old man had learned in seven years.

I became a Christian when I was a student at university, and I have no doubt that this was in part motivated by a degree of 'father hunger.' God used that to draw me to himself. There was a desire for identity and security.

I did not look at all like my adoptive father, being unusually tall and thin. It came as a shock to me when I had children of my own to realise how physically and emotionally like me they were – not just in looks but in mannerisms. Not knowing my biological father there is a sense in which I do not know who I am, or who I will become. When asked for my medical history, for example for insurance applications, I don't have any. I don't know what genetic risk I have for cancer or Alzheimer's, nor whether I should expect my hair to fall out with advancing years.

John takes his deeply moving personal story as the starting point for a theological exploration of the importance of fatherhood. Drawing from a wide range of personal testimonies, many heartbreaking, he shows the damage that fatherlessness causes to individuals and society more widely. Whether a result of unknown fathers, absent fathers or abusive fathers, many of our contemporary problems can be traced back to fatherlessness. This is confirmed by multiple strands of evidence from the social sciences.

John explains why this should not surprise us but rather resonates with the heart of the Christian faith. The Christian revelation of God is of a loving Heavenly Father who adopts us into his family. Human fatherhood is intended to reflect his perfect Fatherhood.

John ably expounds and applies what the Bible has to say about both human fathers and God as father. Helpful personal applications are drawn from this biblical theology of fatherhood, with accompanying questions and carefully chosen prayers that the reader can use. He does not shy away from difficult issues of abuse but offers hope and healing in Christ for those who have been broken and damaged by their human fathers.

For much of my life I realise I have been searching for a substitute father figure and have often been disappointed. In part I have tended to expect more from others than it is fair to ask or expect. John's book is an encouragement to find comfort and security in the only father who can truly satisfy and meet our deepest needs.

I am thankful that John has written this much needed book. It will be a spiritual balm to those who have experienced fatherlessness. It will help those who have been blessed to have fantastic human fathers to understand the pain and needs of those who have not. It will help Christians to share the good news of the gospel with confidence and grace, knowing that they have a point of contact with everyone, because everyone has need of a perfect loving father that cannot be satisfied by any other human being. The gospel is good news for every person, and for society more generally. This book will spur Christian men on to aspire to be better fathers, both to their biological children and their spiritual children in the church family, reflecting something more of the character of their own heavenly father, and seeking his grace for their failings.

John has made himself vulnerable in writing this book with such openness. I would invite you to make yourself vulnerable as you read, allowing God to work in you by his Spirit to heal and transform. His work may feel painful, opening old wounds and places in your soul that may have been kept closed for years, but his purpose is to do you good and grow you to a greater wholeness and happiness, preparing for an eternity enjoying his loving fatherhood in the new creation.

John Stevens
National Director FIEC

Introduction

ABBA is the name of one of the biggest selling pop groups in human history.

The name ABBA comes from the first initials of the four members – Agnetha Fältskog, Benny Andersson, Björn Ulvaeus and Anni-Frid Lyngstad. The band came to the world's attention when they won the Eurovision Song Contest in 1974 for Sweden. Their catchy but complex back catalogue has been hugely popular, providing iconic anthems for a generation, and the soundtrack for a West End musical and two Hollywood blockbusters, *Mamma Mia* and *Mamma Mia: Here We Go Again*.[1] The latter is one of the most popular films of the first two decades of the twenty-first century. Set on an island paradise and building on the phenomenal success of *Mamma Mia*, this film, which is a kind of prequel and sequel rolled into one, is set after the death of Donna, played by Meryl Streep in the first film. The narrative skilfully switches back and forth between 1979 and the twenty-first century. The actress Lily James plays the younger version of Donna, reliving the events that led her to meet daughter Sophie's three possible fathers! This is a film that puts a

---

1 These songs have come alive in a fresh way in 2022 with the phenomenal live show in London that uses computer generated technology to recreate a life-like live concert by the band.

smile on the face, but as a parent I couldn't help but think how horrified I might be if Donna was my daughter!

Like the first film, *Mamma Mia: Here We Go Again* explores the complex nature of identity in a situation where people are coping with real loss. Donna's daughter Sophie is expecting her first baby but Donna, who has recently died, is no longer around to share the joy. A defining feature of Abba's style is the way they wrote sad songs wrapped up in La La Land-like exuberance and glitter. They have been described as some of the most uplifting gloomy songs ever written. ABBA songs relate a narrative of pain, betrayal, and disappointment. Many of their songs like 'Knowing me, Knowing you', face up to the pain of couples breaking up. The two married couples who made ABBA both broke up and were divorced. Many ABBA songs declare that very often life sucks! The songs ask questions but provide very few answers. They explore shattered dreams and broken hearts. One of the songs especially written for the ABBA Voyage experience looks back wistfully at the more harmonious days when both couples were happily married.

It is interesting to note that the film does have more than a faint echo in the life of one of the band members: Anni-Frid Lyngstad, better known simply as Frida was, in fact, not Swedish like the rest of the band members. Frida was born November 15, 1945, in Ballangen outside of Narvik, Norway. Her father was Alfred Haase, a German soldier, and her mother, Synni Lyngstad, was a Norwegian teenager. Frida's father left Norway before Frida was born and was thought to have vanished when his ship was sunk on the way back to Germany.[2] Children like Frida were known as one of the Tyskerbarnas (or 'German children'); Tyskerbarnas and their mothers were ostracised and the child often given up for forced adoption. It was a time of great hostility towards any

---

[2] https://abbasite.com/people/anni-frid-lyngstad/ accessed on Tuesday 5th October 2021.

Norwegians who had had dealings with the Germans. To escape this, her grandmother took Frida to Sweden, her mother joining them later.

Following the death of her mother soon after, Frida was raised by her grandmother. She grew up believing that her father drowned when his ship back to Germany sank. But this proved to be false. In 1977, at the height of ABBA's popularity, Frida and her father were reunited in Switzerland. Their meeting, despite being cordial, did not lead to a sustained relationship, 'It would have been different if I'd been a child. But it's difficult to get a father when you're 32 years old,' Lyngstad explained. 'I can't really connect to him and love him the way I would have if he'd been around when I grew up.'[3] Frida's story highlights how complex fatherlessness can be. The Spoken Word Poetess, Blair Linne has written about the impact on her life of an absent father, 'My home has an absent space, a ghost in our pictures, there is a missing puzzle piece I can never find.'[4]

Yes, that sums it up perfectly: an absent space, a ghost, a missing puzzle piece. There is a hole where Dad should be. He has gone missing. Can that hole ever be filled? Some suggest that fatherlessness creates a hole that is never entirely mended. This book explores the reasons for, and the implications of, that hole, it reflects on the lasting wounds of fatherlessness, and it seeks to feel the impact of being part of a fatherless generation. I sometimes think that being fatherless is like having some wires missing from the circuit of our lives. Some buttons that should work do not do so because they have never been connected. The following chapters will look at some stories of fatherlessness, including my own story, against the backdrop of what the Bible has to say about the subject of fathers and fatherlessness. It also seeks to find ways of experiencing the Fatherhood of God and the phenomenon that

---

3   https://www.biography.com/musician/anni-frid-lyngstad, accessed on Tuesday 5th October 2021.
4   In the poem *Finding My Father*, https://www.youtube.com/watch?v=hx4DS5-NGaE, accessed on Friday 19th July 2024.

is the family of God. The church can go some way to fill that hole, heal those wounds and rewire our circuitry.

This book has been simmering under the surface of my life for decades. It is the fruit of listening to many people's stories and reflecting on my own in the light of Scripture. It would be easy to write a whole book rehearsing the negatives related to fathers and fatherlessness, but I want to try to introduce a fresh breeze of hope into our thinking.

It is important to remember that ABBA is not only the name of a massively popular band, it is also the biblical word that Jesus used when talking to his Father, and which he invites us to use when talking to God. Here is hope for a fatherless world; it is possible to use the word 'father' with freedom rather than fear, with joy rather than disappointment.

Our study here follows a logical path. Firstly to explore what it means to be fatherless and why it matters. Then our biblical reflections begin by examining human fathers in the Old Testament, showing the weaknesses of people and the arrows of hope God gives amidst their failings. We then hear from our contemporaries, seeing how fatherlessness has lasting consequences. As the sorrows caused by human sin and behaviour show our need for a perfect father, we will therefore consider God the Father in the Old Testament, in whom we can find security and identity. We will continue to hear from our contemporaries at intervals, hearing about their different experiences of fatherlessness, before reflecting on what we may learn from human fathers in the New Testament. Our study on God the Father in the New Testament will encourage us again to have confidence in the wonderful, deep love of our Heavenly Father. Our last chapters show us how we must point one another to turn to God, not only for the spiritual fatherhood we all need, but for the comfort and restoration he alone can provide.

'Father had an extraordinary capacity for amiable inattention.' (Frank O'Connor)

'Such is our longing for absent fathers – the father who left, opening up black holes in the fabric of a child's universe, along with the fathers who stayed but whose mercurial distance made them absent even when present. So many people on the road are looking for their fathers.' (JKA Smith)

'The section on my birth certificate reserved for my father's name is blank.' (Blair Linne)

'If you took the love of all the best fathers who've lived, all their goodness, kindness, fidelity, tenderness, strength and united all those qualities in a single person, their love would only be a faint shadow of the furious love in the heart of God the Father for you.' (Brennan Manning)

Chapter 1:
What is it to be fatherless?

I might as well come clean: this is personal. This is not a story about a vague social problem. I am not looking in as a concerned but detached observer. This is my story, this is my wound, and my missing piece.

This came home to me when I arrived somewhat blurry-eyed after an overnight trip that ended at Bujumbura airport in Burundi in 2010 and was presented with a form in French. The question that stared out at me was: Name of Father? My answer 'unknown' seems like an odd answer but it is far from being a rare one. Britain is increasingly becoming a fatherless society with people growing up without knowing their natural father. It happens for a variety of reasons, but what is plain is that you can't rip out of a life such a significant relationship without some sense of real loss, a fatherhood deficit, an aching void that will not easily be filled.

Growing up in the 1960s I assumed that I was the only person who didn't have a father. Everyone seemed to have a full set of parents and a normal family life. Of course, this was not the case then, and it is not the case today. It is important to celebrate the many good fathers who have healthy relationships with their children, but they are becoming a rarer breed. I bump into so many people who have father issues of one kind or another. One of the things that I sensed when I moved to the South

Coast of England in 1997 to become the pastor of Lancing Tabernacle, was that I would be ministering to many fatherless people. And over time, I have become more willing to talk about my own father deficit even though it can be a difficult topic for me to speak about.

There are different ways a child can be fatherless

Some fathers are unknown
A one-night stand, a passing drunken fumble or the victim of rape. The only contribution that some men make as fathers is the transmission of semen. The quickest sperm is the last meaningful contact between father and child.

Some fathers are absent
Away on business, on duty in the armed forces, or have simply disappeared. Many children live with the daily reality that their dads are not there for them. Although there appears to be a strong masculine urge to father children there does not seem to be a corresponding desire among all men to be fathers to those children.

Some fathers are present but distant
Many dads know what it is to be present at the dinner table with their children, but their head and heart are in another place.

I like to listen to BBC Radio 4's *Desert Island Discs*. It has been striking how many of the castaways speak about struggling with an absent, distant or dysfunctional father. Sir Keir Starmer, the former head of the Department of Public Prosecution, and current Prime Minister, said, 'I don't often talk about my dad … He was a difficult man, a complicated man, he kept himself to himself, he didn't particularly like to socialise, so wouldn't really go out very much. But he was incredibly hard-working …

I wouldn't say we were close. I understood who he was and what he was, but we weren't close, and I regret that.'[1]

Germaine Greer, the feminist writer, tells of how she took home a report from school and although all her results were excellent apart from maths, her Dad's only comment was, 'What happened to maths?'

Reading the lives of many famous singers from Bono to Bruce Springsteen it has been interesting to observe how many have had issues with their fathers. Much of Springsteen's career seems to be defined by a search for intimacy and approval from his father. For Bono, the lead singer of the Irish band U2, there was between him and his father, rivalry, distance, and mystery. 'My father was a tenor, a really, really good one.'[2] For all Bono's success as a singer, he never felt that he measured up to the quality of his dad's voice. Bono describes himself as 'A tenor out front who can't accept he's a baritone. A small man singing giant songs.' Bono and his dad were distant: 'To be close as a father shouldn't be so easy for me, because I wasn't that close to mine.'[3]

This distance was made worse by the death of Bono's mother when he was only fourteen. Added to this was the mystery that the man he thought was his cousin, was in fact his half-brother.

Frank Turner is a singer who came to public attention through his appearance at the opening ceremony of the 2012 Olympic Games in London. His latest album FTHR includes the song 'Fatherless', that explores the painful sense of distance and lack of interest he felt from his father, particularly being sent off to boarding school at the age of eight years old. Winston Churchill also speaks of his pain as a small boy being shipped off to boarding school as a further nail in the coffin of

---

1 *Desert Island Discs* 15/11/2020.
2 Bono, *Surrender: 40 Songs, one story*, (Hutchinson-Heinemann: London, 2022) p.31.
3 Bono, *Surrender*, p.523.

his almost non-existent relationship with his father.[4] Turner sings about selling his soul to Rock and Roll in a desperate attempt to be noticed. In a bizarre twist another song on the album is entitled 'Miranda', which is the name by which Turner's father now identifies as a trans-woman. Ironically this twist makes Turner, an LGBTI+ sympathiser, able to feel reconciled to his father. The story is a reminder of the complex implications of fatherlessness in the twenty-first century.[5]

Some fathers are present but abusive

This abuse can take the form of harsh words, quick fists or unwelcome sexual advances. The latter is perhaps the most confusing because it is so unnatural. This is not the kind of attention that a father should be giving his children.[6]

Another Desert Island castaway was Ian Wright, the former Arsenal and England footballer, who speaks about his relationship with his stepfather. Ironically when this phenomenal footballer was growing up his father would not let him watch *Match of the Day* but forced him to stand with his back to the television facing the opposite wall.[7]

The comedian David Sedaris's father described his son in the following way: 'You are a big fat zero.' Sedaris says that: 'As long as my dad had power, he used it to hurt me.'[8]

Singer songwriter Richard Thompson writes of his experience of fear:

---

4 Andrew Roberts, *Churchill: Walking with Destiny*, (Allen Lane: London, 2018) p.p. 7–31.
5 https://www.theguardian.com/music/2021/nov/25/frank-turner-on-reconciling-with-his-trans-parent-miranda-is-a-really-nice-person-my-dad-wasnt accessed 18/12/2024
6 See Chapter 5 ~ Interview: Mending the Broken Hallelujah. ~ Child abuse
7 Ian Wright on *Desert Island Discs* 16/02/2020
8 *Desert Island Discs* 12/02/2023.

I was very shy, and from around the age of six I developed a stutter. The causes of this are not always clear – my mother thought it started for me after a bout of dysentery, but there was probably a psychological factor. I lived in fear of my father, who was sometimes drunk and always Calvinistic – a common Scottish combination – so I never knew when I was going to get whacked.[9]

Some fathers leave us too soon

This is a particular issue in the aftermath of war when those who die in combat or the crossfire leave children behind that they may not even have met. This aching void is also experienced by those who have lost their fathers through terminal illness or a tragic accident. People in these circumstances talk about living in a story either where the final chapters are ripped out or full of blank pages where shared conversations and experiences would have been recorded.[10]

People experience the death of their fathers differently. This sometimes results in a wistful: 'I wish my dad were still here to see this', leading to 'Why on earth did you have to die so young?' Among my friends, I know those who lost their dads before they were born, before they were old enough to really know them, or months before their wedding or before they began to take their own path in their career. Hannah Beckman writes of the death of her father in a different tone:

> It was October 2018 when I received the news that I'd been anticipating for some time. My father had died ... I had been estranged from him for almost 25 years: my entire adult life ... I do not remember a time when I wasn't fearful of him. As an alcoholic, he was prone to outbursts of violent temper, often veering from ebullient drunkenness to inebriated abuse without a moment's

---

9 Richard Thompson Beeswing, *Losing My Way and Finding My Voice 1967-1975* (Algonquin Books: London, 2022) p. 7.
10 See Chapter 9 – Interviews: Lost Too Early.

warning. His vitriol could be directed at anyone ... There's something profoundly destabilising about growing up in a state of permanent unpredictability: not knowing which drunken version – the exuberant or the enraged – would come through the door each evening.

When I left ... I was relinquishing the very notion of having a good father in my life. I was giving up hope – however misplaced – that he might be able to change, to transform himself, like a character in a fairy-tale, into someone kind, caring and affectionate. I was in essence, accepting that I would never have something that all children deserve, two functioning loving parents. This is why I did not grieve his death ... Psychologically for me, my father died long before he passed away.[11]

Why it matters: the effects of being fatherless

Whatever the reason for a person being fatherless, there are knock-on effects in their lives. There is the sense that something is missing, there is a hole where a father's love should be. How does a person recover from this? Is there a way back at all? This is an important question for three reasons.

1. Such a father deficit has an impact on our sense of identity. Human beings are people in relationships. Much of who we consider ourselves to be is derived from the connected relationships that have formed us.
2. Father deficits in our lives tend to shape our own attitude to parenting. Having a relational hole in our lives means that there is something missing in our knowledge and experience. It is like faulty wiring that makes meaningful connection difficult.

---

[11] Hannah Beckman, 'Cutting ties with my father was the best thing I ever did', i paper, Monday 9th January 2023, p.35.

3. A human father deficit can have an impact on the way that we think about God. JB Philips describes this as a 'parental hangover' and says 'Many Psychologists assure us that the trend of the whole of a man's life is largely determined by his attitude in early years toward his parents.'[12]

The guitarist Eric Clapton grew up being very close to his older sister. It was not until he was an adult that he discovered that his 'sister' was in fact his mother. She had got pregnant during the Second World War, in a relationship with a Canadian airman she had met at a local dance. After the war the airman returned to Canada, leaving behind one of many fatherless children. To protect her from shame, her parents hatched up the story about Eric being his grandmother's child.

Clapton wrote about his father in the poignant song: 'My Father's Eyes'. The song was inspired by the fact that Clapton never met his father, Edward Fryer, who died of leukaemia in 1985. The song describes how he wished he had met his father and refers to his own son Conor, who died in 1991 at age four after falling from the 53rd floor of the New York City apartment of his mother. The song relates how the closest he gets to looking into his father's eyes is looking into the eyes of his son. Every fatherless child consciously or unconsciously is longing to look into their father's eyes, to find the missing piece and to heal the open wound. We are made for connection and when that connection is broken or missing the pain can be unbearable.

Eugene Peterson, the author of the bestselling paraphrase of the Bible, *The Message*, talks to his biographer about his relationship with his father. Peterson 'could not remember his dad hugging him or ever saying "I love you" or "I'm proud of you." '[13] Instead Peterson talks about 'the hole where a father's love was supposed to rest.'

---

12 JB Philips, *Your God is too Small*, (Epworth Press: London, 1952), p.18.
13 Winn Collier, *A Burning in my Bones, The Authorised Biography of Eugene H. Peterson*, (Authentic: London, 2021), p.21.

The knock-on effect of this was that Peterson found it difficult to emotionally engage with his own son Eric. Eric wrote his Dad a letter outlining what was missing in their relationship. Eugene read the letter through tears and responded in the following way: 'I'm so sorry Eric. I didn't realise how much I've done to you what my dad did to me. I'm sorry.'

Eric reflected on his relationship with his Dad:

> My dad learned how to be a dad from his dad. We all have father wounds ... I love my dad. I'm proud of him: proud of who he is, what he's done, and proud to be his son. But that's not the point. The point is that I am missing something in my life because he didn't give it to me. And I need to learn how to recover it, or at least how to resolve the conflict I am experiencing.'[14]

When I look in the mirror, I see a person I have never met and a face I have never seen. When I think of the idea of a father, I am confronted with a massive question mark. I was reminded of this when watching a TV programme to mark the 70th anniversary of Victory in Europe Day. It was a programme in which several famous people recalled the events of that day back in May 1945. Two stories were particularly interesting to me. One was about Patrick Stewart, of *Star Trek* fame, who spoke with affection for the war years spent with his mother and brother at home. Then came the shock of their domestic calm being invaded by an 'unknown' man, who was his father. Stewart's father had been used to having a role and a position in the army but in civilian life he was just a nobody. He was authoritarian, distant and troubled; during the week he worked at what felt like a non-job, at the weekend he became (in an attempt to deal with the effects of severe shell shock) a reclusive weekend alcoholic.

---

14 Winn Collier, *A Burning in my Bones*, p.163.

The other story was about John Craven, who was a newsreader for the BBC, most famous for the innovative children's programme, *John Craven's Newsround*. He speaks of being puzzled at VE day because his father, who was a prisoner of war in the Far East, had not returned home. The war was yet to end there, and it would be some time before they would be sure that his father was alive and would be coming home. When the day finally came, he went with his mother to meet his father. Years working on the Death Railway in Burma had taken its toll, and Craven says that his father was no more than skin and bone; yet when he saw his son's face he picked him up and put him on his shoulders and carried him home. Maybe it was something about the face of his son that made him grateful to be home and gave him hope and a purpose. Faces are the most distinctive thing about us; they communicate identity.

My experience of being fatherless

The first faces I remember are the faces of my mother and my grandmother; I say grandmother, even though she was not actually a relative. My mother's mother had died when my mother was three years old, and for some reason, which I have never really understood, my 'grandmother' and her husband took her in. At 16 my mum was living in London, an innocent abroad, and was probably fairly naïve. Nine months later I was born at St John's hospital in Chelmsford.

I spent my first year in mother and baby homes attached to convents in Chelmsford and Wales before moving back to Lowestoft to move in with my 'grandmother'. We made an odd family: teenage single mother, an unrelated middle-aged Scottish woman (with no children of her own) and a toddler!

The years that followed brought one very short-lived marriage, a succession of uncles, and three more children: Peter, Paul and Mary. For some reason they were taken away for adoption. I still remember their puzzled faces as they were taken away. I stayed and when I was about ten years old one of the uncles became my stepfather. He was a seaman, which meant that he was away most of the time and in the pub when back on shore; we did not have much of a relationship. In an attempt to get me onside, he claimed that he was my real father. This was ridiculous as he was younger than my mother and still a schoolboy in Cornwall when I was born. On one occasion he became angry with me and chased me around the garden with a broken bottle in his hand; thankfully I could move quickly!

When I was in my teens my mum had three other children, Maria, Bobby, and Daniel. It was not easy having this background. Many parents didn't want their children to hang out with me or to visit our house. I remember a birthday party that was organised for me when none of the children invited turned up. We sometimes used to have cruel notes put through the letterbox, sometimes accompanied by a packet of dog's mess. I became used to disapproving faces.

Yet two faces from my school days stay with me: Mr Stephen Payne and Mr John Sanham.[15] John was my Maths Teacher (sorry John, Maths simply did not add up for me!), Stephen was my Religious Education teacher. They were both Christians and led the popular Christian Union at the School. I went along and was interested in what they said, even attending some of their weekends away.

There has never been a point in my life when I have not believed in God. As I have said I spent my first year in accommodation provided by convents and was baptised in the Catholic Church. My 'grandmother' was brought up in the Scottish Presbyterian Church but seemed to spend her life searching for something. We had some neighbours who were Mormons. My vivid memory of them was drinking cocoa poured

---

15 Stephen and John were both members of Beresford Road Evangelical Church. This is where I became a Christian and was baptised. Ten years after my first visit to the church in 1972 I was ordained its first pastor on 1st April 1982. It was a great joy to appoint John as one of my elders during my fifteen years there as pastor.

from a teapot. 'Grandmother' took me along to the Mormon Church and was baptised as a Mormon. But like a true Scot she baulked at the demand for a 10% weekly offering! I was sent to the local evangelical church Sunday School. My attendance was patchy. After one very long absence I returned with the story that I had had the measles! Then 'grandmother' began to talk to the Jehovah's Witnesses: one elderly couple (who also had no children) were very kind to us, having us around for tea and teaching me to play board games. I believed in God, but I can see now that these were false paths, I had not yet come face to face with the truth.

Something needed to happen to jolt me and grab my attention. One of my classmates turned up in class one day with a booklet entitled *Jesus is Alive*. This was quite a surprise as his main interest in life was radical left-wing politics. Every Saturday he could be found trying to sell the *Socialist Worker* outside our local Odeon Cinema. Seeing my incredulity, he said: 'Come along to our youth group tonight and see what you think.' I did go that evening. Here, packed into the front room of a modern town house, were young people of my age who were excited about God. I was impressed by what I had seen: when they read the Bible it was as if they were listening to the voice of a friend, when they prayed, it was as if they were talking to a real person, and when they sang it was as if they were engaging face to face with the living God. When the host dropped me back home that evening, I asked him how I could know God like that. He explained the gospel to me, I went into my house and for the first time in my life addressed someone as Father, and suddenly the distance collapsed between the God I believed existed and the God I could know personally.

Near the beginning of the 21st century a radio show asked its listeners to sum up the Christian message in a sentence. The best result was a fresh take on The Monkees' song from the 1960s, *I'm a Believer*, made famous again for a new generation in the film *Shrek*: 'Then I saw *his* face:

now I'm a believer!' (my italics). This is not a million miles away from how the Apostle Paul puts it:

> For God who said: "Let light shine out of darkness", made his light shine in our hearts to give us the light of the knowledge of God's glory displayed in the face of Christ. (2 Cor. 4:6)

The face of Jesus has revealed the Father's glory. The privilege of becoming a son of God was the greatest blessing imaginable to me! As a 16-year-old it was so liberating that for the first time in my life I was able to call another person Father. The Holy Spirit, God's empowering presence, gave me freedom to know God with astonishing intimacy: 'rather, the Spirit you received brought about your adoption to sonship. And by him we cry, "Abba, Father." ' (Rom. 8:15) An everyday term used by small children is used to address the Creator of the Universe. How astonishing that I, the fatherless John, can without hesitation or inhibition use the prayer language used by Jesus (Mk. 14:36) to speak to God.

Yet I need to be clear about this: such a discovery did not resolve all of my questions, nor did it fill the fatherhood deficit I had in my life. I have not resolved the mystery of my unknown father, the unknown name and the unseen face, but my heart is in the process of being healed and I have gained a life-changing relationship with my heavenly Father. The Psalmist asserts with confidence: 'Though my father and mother forsake me, the LORD will receive me.' (Ps. 27:10)

As Blair Linne writes: 'Having God as Father doesn't take away all of the pain of not having our biological dad, but it does help us wrestle through that pain and come out on the other side more dependent upon our unchanging Father.'[16]

---

16 Blair Linne, *Finding My Father: How the Gospel Heals the Pain of Fatherlessness*, (The Good Book Company: London, 2021), p.149.

Sometimes I will conclude a service with the words of the ancient blessing recorded in the Book of Numbers.

"The LORD bless you
    and keep you;
the LORD make his face shine on you
    and be gracious to you;
the LORD turn his face toward you
    and give you peace." ' (Num. 6:24-26)

I love the sense of movement in these words as they promise that this personal God will keep us, be gracious and give us peace. All these blessings flow from the glowing face of the Father who has been made known to us in Jesus his Son. This is at the beating heart of what our heavenly Father wants to share with us through the giving of his one and only Son: 'The Son of God became the Son of Man so that the sons and daughters of men might become the sons and daughters of God.'[17]

Amen to that! What a game changer that is. I am not a nobody. I am not a blank line on a brief certificate. I am not an orphan, I am not a slave, I am a son, and *he* is my Father. Yet I, like many of the fatherless, have issues, some visible, some hidden in plain sight, and some buried deep that continue to make it harder to be who I am meant to be. This book is an attempt to shine fresh light on this issue.

Questions:

1) If you have had a healthy relationship with a good father: what do you most appreciate about that relationship?

2) If for one reason or another you are fatherless: what have you discovered in your life that is helpful for mending the wound, and in

---

17 Attributed in one form or another to one of the early Church Fathers.

what areas of your life are you still experiencing that loss as an open wound?

Prayer:

Father God:
You are the answer to the longings of my aching heart.
You are the healing balm that heals my relational wounds.
You are the one who promises to wipe away all tears.
You are the face that shines on me with gracious tenderness and peace.
Help me to find in you my significance, sufficiency and security.
Help me to discover my true identity through knowing you.
In Jesus' name. Amen.

Action

Find wise and practical ways to learn how to support those who experience different forms of fatherlessness.

'"Fatherhood" is embedded in the warp and woof of Old Testament theology.' (The Dictionary of Biblical Imagery)

'Our past is not past; it oozes into the present. Skeletons in the closet from generations past still drip, drip, drip into our lives.' (James K. A. Smith)

Chapter 2:
Human fathers in the biblical story ~ Old Testament

We begin with human fathers rather than God as Father because it is the former that is addressed first in the biblical record. The initial stories of the later part of Genesis (chapters 12 – 50) are those of the Patriarchs or fathers.

In fact (Ab), אָב, the Hebrew word for father, is the first word in the Hebrew Dictionary. This might simply be a linguistic accident, but it does put the word for father upfront and central to the Hebrew language and the biblical story. It is clear, simple, and foundational. The word is described as: 'an onomatopoeic word imitating the babbling sounds of an infant i.e., as a child's word.'[1]

The concept of the father in the Bible includes not only the immediate male ancestor but also more distant ancestors. In a metaphorical sense, father may refer to a founder or an authority figure. The father served as a protector, responsible for the education and well-being of the family.

The man chosen and called to become the Father of Israel and the Father of those who have faith is called Abram (Father).[2] That name is extended to Abraham (Father of many), because he will be the 'father

---

[1] *Theological Dictionary of the Old Testament*, Edited by G. Johannes Botterwick and Helmer Ringgren, Translated by John T. Willis, Vol. 1, (Eerdmans, 1974), p.1.
[2] Gen. 12:1–3

of many nations', which is the meaning of the lengthening of his name after the covenant of circumcision.[3] It seems that we are supposed to pay attention to this label that becomes a defining concept for understanding God's dealings with human beings throughout history.

There are many examples of human father figures in the Scriptures from Adam through to Joseph, the earthly father of Jesus. There are no clear role models of good fathers in the Old Testament (with the possible exceptions of Enoch and Job).

The Old Testament contains story after story of fathers who fail. Yet we need to be careful here. Biblical narrative is not moralistic. It does not generally engage in reflective commentary on what it records, therefore we need to exercise care before we make negative inferences concerning fathers depicted in Scripture. Care also needs to be taken not to read these stories through the lens of Western middle-class nuclear families, especially if we assume that these neat semi-detached social units are superior to other ways to organise families. Some Christians in cultures where family networks are closer to those recorded in Scripture are horrified by the reduced family on display and celebrated in the West.

Clearly there is going to be a difference between a father who has two children and a father like Gideon, who had seventy sons. The modern language of parental bonding and relationships cannot be superimposed on the Bible as a norm against which all behaviour of biblical characters is measured. At many points there is not a clear like-for-like comparison.

Adam

Adam is the first human father in Scripture. Although it is questionable to argue from silence, what are we to make of Adam's relationship with

---

3 Gen. 17:5

his sons Cain and Abel? Apart from the record of their conception there is no hint of interaction between father and sons.

In the extended account of the birth of Adam's son Seth in Genesis 5:1–3, the writer of Genesis plays with the idea of being made in the image of God. Adam is made in God's image; Seth is made in Adam's image. The idea of humans being made in God's image is not completely lost after the Fall (see Gen. 9:5–6) but that image is at best marred. Humans continue to bear the marks of dust and glory but often that glory is heavily disguised.

What does it mean to say that Seth is made in Adam's image? Perhaps it means that he has something of the imprint of Adam on him. Every child has some imprint of their fathers on them even if the only contribution a man has made is the sperm that fertilised the egg in their mother's womb.

Cain, Adah, Jubal, Seth

The first men to actually be called fathers are described in Genesis 4:20–21.

> Adah gave birth to Jabal; he was the father of those who live in tents and raise livestock. His brother's name was Jubal; he was the father of all who play stringed instruments and pipes.

Two fascinating micro narratives are crammed into these sparse descriptions of the fathers of nomadic farmers and the fathers of musicians. They hint that fathers in the ancient world have a strong influence on lifestyle, location, careers, trades and cultural pursuits. The custom of having a surname that reflected a person's work might be an extension of this. Originally if you were called Baker, Butcher, Carpenter, Miller or Plumber it indicated what your family did. Fathers passed down skills, knowledge and values to their children.

Cain, Adam and his son Seth are spoken of as having sons, but none of them is described as 'being a father.' The father who appears to have the greatest impact on his family and society is Seth. Seth named his son Enosh, which means human being, which probably is a testimony to the frailty of human life. It is perhaps no accident that the author of Genesis says that this birth marked a crucial turning point in human history: 'At that time people began to call on the name of the LORD.' (Gen. 4:26)

This renewed spiritual awareness points the way to the story of Enoch, who is a rare bright spot in an otherwise bleak picture of the human race in general and fathers in particular. Enoch, who is singled out in the portrait gallery of faith (Heb. 11:5) as someone who pleased God, is unique as one of that rare club of biblical characters who does not die. His brief but compelling story of a God-centred life is told amidst a litany of death in Genesis 5.

> When Enoch had lived 65 years, he became the father of Methuselah. After he became the father of Methuselah, Enoch walked faithfully with God 300 years and had other sons and daughters. Altogether, Enoch lived a total of 365 years. Enoch walked faithfully with God; then he was no more, because God took him away. (Gen. 5:21-24)

Enoch is celebrated as a man who combined the ordinary with the extraordinary. He managed to hold together living a productive life, being a dad and maintaining a healthy relationship with God.

> Take Enoch for your father. Take him for your patron patriarch. Take him for your example. Follow him in his blessed footsteps in his family life. It was his first son that made Enoch a saint. As soon as he saw his first child in his image, and in his arms, Enoch became from that day a new man.[4]

---

4 Alexander Whyte, *Bible Characters: The Old Testament*, (London: Oliphants, 1952), p.39.

Many new fathers have an epiphany moment that coincides with the birth of their first child, that unusual almost mystical sense that this is more than the product of a sperm and an egg. For most new fathers the feeling fades quickly; for Enoch it continued forever.

Noah

It was supposed to be a fresh beginning for humanity. The earth had been symbolically cleansed by the flood waters and a fresh covenant had been made with all creation. The story has so much in common with the original creation story. Both Adam and Noah had received a clear creation mandate, engaged in agriculture (both are described as men of the soil, Gen. 2:5; 9:20), experienced broken relationships, and ended up naked and full of shame. This is the first record in the Bible of a father who has gone on a bender and then lived to regret the consequences.

Noah, who had heroically saved his family from disaster by building an ark before the earth was overtaken by a flood, now puts his family in deadly peril. Like many men, Noah discovered that it can sometimes be easier to tackle an external threat than deal with the enemy within.

Noah as a father had the responsibility to protect his family; instead of protecting his sons he exposes them to what they are not supposed to see and opens the door to shame. Two of Noah's three sons go out of their way to protect their father in his drink-fuelled nakedness. The other lingers, looks and is marked forever. There are some things that sons see in the lives of their fathers that they simply cannot un-see. It might be finding their father in bed with another woman, or engaging in an act of violence, dishonesty, or being locked up in jail.

This dishonouring of a good father fractured the relationship and led to distance. The curse is a consequence of this. To fully grasp what is going on here we need to understand the nature of a shame and honour culture and detect the echoes of Eden.[5]

Abraham

Abram, as we have seen, has the image of father imprinted in his name. All of the major incidents in his life flow out of the promise that he is going to have an heir. The fulfilment of this promise seems to be complicated by Abram and Sarah's advanced age.

Anxiety about living long enough to see God's promise fulfilled led to attempts by Abram to engineer a solution. These include the suggestion that his head servant could be his heir and then the choice of another servant to be a surrogate mother. This plan goes disastrously wrong when the surrogate mother and her child become a focus for Sarah's jealousy.

The expulsion of Hagar and her son Ishmael is not Abram's finest hour. It is commanded by God but the way that God has to come to their assistance in the wilderness suggests that the way Abraham deals with the matter has more than a hint of carelessness and cruelty. Here is the first example of a biological child being abandoned by its father. The incident opens a window on the sting of rejection felt by the fatherless.

Genesis 22 records one of the most controversial episodes in the whole Bible. As we have noted, the biblical narrative does not tend to comment negatively on the behaviour of its characters. Yet the chapter contains the shock of God calling on Abraham to sacrifice his only, long awaited, son. A dispassionate reader might well think that a discreet call to Social Services might be in order! Scripture itself is not silent on this

---

5 Some suggest that Ham looking on his father's nakedness is a euphemism for sexual misconduct (Lev. 18), see for example: Adnwarul Azad and Ida Glazer, *Genesis 1-11* (Langham: Carlisle, 2022), p.228. There is no evidence of this in the Genesis account.

issue yet, to the surprise of some, Abraham's actions are labelled as 'by faith'.

> By faith Abraham, when God tested him, offered Isaac as a sacrifice. He who had embraced the promises was about to sacrifice his one and only son, even though God had said to him, "It is through Isaac that your offspring will be reckoned." Abraham reasoned that God could even raise the dead, and so in a manner of speaking he did receive Isaac back from death. (Heb. 11:17–19).

Space does not allow an exploration of the full implications of this story. Yet it is interesting to note that Isaac, apart from his question about where the sacrificial lamb is, does not show any signs of being ill-treated by Abraham or appear to have any reason to distrust his father.

Lot

Lot is Abram's nephew. When his father dies, Abram takes him under his wing. Their paths soon diverged, Abram choosing to follow God's promise of living in Canaan while Lot was attracted to the bright lights of the city of Sodom, a place noted for its sinfulness (Gen. 13:13). This was not a good place to be. In Genesis 14 Lot, who has been sailing too close to the wind, is captured and swept away in a raid on Sodom, and it falls to Abram to marshal his men to rescue him. Abram is offered a reward by the king of Sodom for rescuing Lot and others from the city; Abram refuses.

> But Abram said to the king of Sodom, "With raised hand I have sworn an oath to the LORD, God Most High, Creator of heaven and earth, that I will accept nothing belonging to you, not even a thread or the strap of a sandal, so that you will never be able to say, 'I made Abram rich.' (Gen 14:22–23).

Abram sees the danger of getting too close to a city that so stridently defies God; sadly Lot fails to do so. In Genesis 19 the story is told of Lot continuing to expose his wife and daughters to dangers in Sodom, a place name that is synonymous with chaotic wickedness. The story is full of shocking details of how Lot approached fatherhood.

An astonishing offer (Gen. 19:1-8)
When angelic messengers come to Lot's house to warn him to get out of town quickly, the local men come to ask if they can have sex with them. Lot's shocking solution is to offer his unmarried daughters to them instead.

A man who is not taken seriously (Gen. 19:9-14)
There is always a danger of spending so much time engaging in Dad Jokes that it is difficult for children to know when to take their fathers seriously. If everything in life is a joke, then when an occasion requires seriousness, it is impossible for others to hear us in that register. Lot attempts to rescue his sons-in-law from the impending doom. This attempt fails because they think he is 'joking'. (Gen. 19:14)

Too little too late (Gen. 19:15-26)
The desperate last-minute half-hearted scramble to safety led to the death of his wife, who against angelic instruction looks back just a little too longingly. She ends up as a pillar of salt, like those in Pompei petrified by volcanic ash, in a permanent image of terror. The lack of a timely escape plan results in Lot and his daughters being exposed to even more danger.

Descending to a new low (Gen. 19:30-38)
Lot and his two daughters end up living in a cave. His daughters are full of fear, and desperate to have a future. In the light of their hopeless

situation they make Lot the unwitting apparatus for shaping and seizing a future of their own making. The story of Lot's daughters getting him drunk and being impregnated by him is one of the most shocking accounts recorded in the Old Testament. Lot's role as a father was supposed to be one of protection, care and support, but it turned out to be one of exposure to danger, crushing of hope, and a spiral into loveless lawlessness. A story like this never ends well. This one ends with the birth of two boys who become the fathers of Israel's arch enemies, the Moabites and the Amorites. Ironically the boys' names Moab and Ben-Ammi have reference to their origins.[6]

Isaac

> He is a shadowy figure compared to his father, Abraham, and his son Jacob, but at certain moments in his life the shadows recede about him, and he stands on the stage in a flood of light.[7]

Isaac is depicted in Genesis as a complex transitional figure, who at times appears to be the passive observer in his own story. Waiting for his bride-to-be to arrive with his Father's servant – we are told he 'went out to the field one evening to meditate' (Gen. 24:63). The word used for meditating is not entirely clear, it could be thinking or praying, but it could have been staring or daydreaming. There are hints that there is more to him than meets the eye. Genesis records that as a would-be father, Isaac prays for his childless wife; she conceives and gives birth to twin boys, Esau and Jacob (Gen. 25:21). The Lord also appears to Isaac on at least two occasions (Gen. 26:2–5, 24), yet it is to be noted that the promise of blessing is because of the faithfulness of Abraham.

---

6 Moab sounds like the Hebrew for 'from father'. Ben-Ammi means son of my father's people.
7 Frederick Buechner, *Peculiar Treasures, A Biblical Who's Who*, (Harper Collins: New York, 1979), p.58.

Genesis 26 also records a chilling instance of Isaac being a passive echo of his own father as he repeats the actions of Abraham when confronted with a similar danger (Gen. 12:10-20, 20:1-17; 26:1-11). Isaac was not alive to see his father's duplicity in lying about Sarah being his sister to save his own skin, but it was either passed on through his genes or was something that he picked up by osmosis as he observed Abraham in other settings.

The fatherless child has no idea about the character of their father, so it is a mystery to them whether they take after their father or not. The rock guitarist Eric Clapton, whose story I told earlier, comments that: 'I sometimes wonder what aspects of my character might be shaped by my biological father.' Knowingly or unknowingly fathers leave traces in the lives of their children that can have an impact on how they look, feel, talk and on what they do. Children can inherit temperaments, skills, and health issues from their fathers. This can be a welcome character trait or skill that brings delight, or a negative mindset or medical condition that is like a ticking time bomb that might explode at any moment with disastrous consequences.

Isaac's boys would carry on the promise, but it is worth noting that the key information about their place in the story was not given to Isaac but to their mother, Rebekah. Rebekah had sought the Lord about why the twins has been jostling so violently in her womb:

> The LORD said to her,
> "Two nations are in your womb,
>   and two peoples from within you will be separated;
> one people will be stronger than the other,
>   and the older will serve the younger." (Gen. 25:23)

There is no indication in the story that Rebekah told Isaac about this incident, but this is a vital piece of information for seeing how the story unravels. The almost blind elderly Isaac is duped into giving the blessing of the firstborn to Jacob for a good meal; his eldest son Esau has already sold his birthright to his younger brother for a bowl of stew. Father and son clearly both liked their food a little too much!

Rebekah was aware that the elder son Esau would serve the younger Jacob and engineered things to make sure that this happened. The last recorded fatherly action of Isaac toward Jacob was to offer wise counsel about marriage:

> So Isaac called for Jacob and blessed him. Then he commanded him: "Do not marry a Canaanite woman. Go at once to Paddan Aram, to the house of your mother's father Bethuel. Take a wife for yourself there, from among the daughters of Laban, your mother's brother. May God Almighty bless you and make you fruitful and increase your numbers until you become a community of peoples. May he give you and your descendants the blessing given to Abraham, so that you may take possession of the land where you now reside as a foreigner, the land God gave to Abraham." Then Isaac sent Jacob on his way, and he went to Padden Aram, to Laban son of Bethuel the Aramean, the brother of Rebekah, who was the mother of Jacob and Esau. (Gen. 28:1–5)

The downside of this was that Esau, having heard of this blessing and consumed by bitterness, broke his parents' hearts with an inappropriate marriage to a Canaanite woman. It also meant that Jacob had to run for his life, leaving home, never to see the face of his mother again, and only seeing his father a short time before his death.

This part of the biblical narrative appears to be something akin to a soap opera, with the four main characters Isaac, Rebekah, Esau, and Jacob functioning as semi-detached individuals, who interact without any significant interpersonal connection. This is one of the points in the story of the promise, when that promise seems to be at its most precarious! The sacred narrative descends at points to tragicomedy, not least when Jacob dupes his father with props from the dressing-up box.

Jacob

The Dictionary of Biblical Imagery suggests that Jacob's upbringing and experience was lived out in how he parented his own children. Jacob clearly has his favourites, notably Rachel's boys, Joseph and Benjamin. The gift to Joseph of a 'coat of many colours' led to bitterness and jealousy that resulted in ten of Jacob's sons almost leaving Joseph for dead, before selling him into slavery.

Joseph is sent by Jacob to see his brothers, who are looking after livestock at some distance away. Jacob must have known that his treating Joseph as his favourite, the coat, and Joseph's bold dreams had made the others jealous. I wonder if it had occurred to Jacob to say to Joseph: 'Perhaps it might be best to leave that coat behind.'

When Jacob dies there is extraordinary grief not merely because of the great patriarch's death, but also because Joseph's brothers assume that now Jacob is gone Joseph will have revenge for their cruel treachery. It is a sad reality that the death of a father can pitch the whole family into inconsolable grief, financial instability, and relational breakdown.

Joseph's brothers anticipate this potential danger and report to Joseph what they suggest Jacob had said about his desire for Joseph to forgive his brothers (Gen. 50:15-18). This intervention proved to be unnecessary because Joseph echoes his original words of forgiveness (Gen. 50:19-21, c.f. Gen. 45:4-11). Jacob had given a lengthy blessing to his sons as recorded in Genesis 49 but there is no other evidence that he had made a request for Joseph to forgive his brothers.

Judah

One of the darkest episodes in Jacob's family shows something of their attitude to fatherhood. The incident involves the daughter-in-law of Jacob's son, Judah. The story of Tamar is recorded in Genesis 38. This is another story of a desperate woman taking matters into her own hands.

Tamar's husband has died, and his brother has refused to marry her, in accordance with custom in order to give his dead brother an heir. Perhaps Tamar had not read the research that suggests that most men think about sex every seven minutes but she knew enough about the predictability of men to lay a trap for Judah. She dresses as a shrine prostitute and waits at the roadside, where she knows that Judah will be passing. Predictably he is attracted to his daughter-in-law in disguise, has sex with her, and not having any cash on him, promises her a young goat for her services and leaves his seal, cord, and staff as pledge of future payment. It was almost like leaving his credit card details as a guarantee of payment.

The next day he tries to pay his debt but finds no shrine prostitute by the side of the road and the people there say that there is no such woman in these parts. Judah is too embarrassed to make a fuss and tries to forget about the 'transaction' and the possible outcome of the 'sowing of his wild oats'. When the news gets out that Tamar is pregnant, she is in great danger, until she is able to produce the seal, cord staff, and thus obtain justice.

There are millions of stories of babies who have been born after a relatively anonymous encounter. After the sex, some men have no further interest in the woman or any child that might result from their encounter.

Louise Perry cites Sherry Argov, concerning two distinct approaches men take to women they meet:

> What men don't want women to know is that, almost immediately, they put women into one of two categories: "good time only" or "worthwhile"... Men in 'cad' mode aren't concerned with the welfare of their unknown offspring, since they are favouring quantity over

quality, but men in 'dad' mode care a great deal and will often devote their lives to providing for their families.[8]

The categories of cad and dad do seem to describe Judah's approach to Tamar, first in his callous treatment of her, and then in his eventual overdue support for her.

Job

The story of Job seems to fit into the patriarchal period. The beginning and the end of the book of Job provide snapshots of Job's approach to fatherhood. At the beginning we are told that he made his seven sons and three daughters a spiritual priority in his life. It tells of how the children would gather together to celebrate their birthdays:

> When a period of feasting had run its course, Job would make arrangements for them to be purified. Early in the morning he would sacrifice a burnt offering for each of them, thinking, "Perhaps my children have sinned and cursed God in their hearts." This was Job's regular custom. (Job 1:5)

The book of Job continues with the puzzling and devastating loss of all ten of Job's children. When at the end of the story he has another ten children, he treats them with such delight, dignity and generosity, even granting his daughters a share of the inheritance (Job 42:13-15).

> The clearest expression of the renewal of Job's mind is not anything he says. It is his willingness to have more children. I have heard it said in modern Israel that the most courageous act of faith the

---

8 Louise Perry, *The Case Against the Sexual Revolution: A New Guide to Sex in the 21st Century*, (Polity: London, 2022), p.121.

Jews have ever performed was to have babies after the Holocaust, to trust God with more defenceless children.[9]

Moses, Aaron and Joshua

There is very little detail about these men as fathers, but Aaron's sons, who follow him into priesthood are put to death for offering 'unauthorized fire' before God (Num. 3:4) and are killed outright by God before they had sons themselves. Out of these three it is Joshua who is most emphatic about his attitude to fatherhood. His strong affirmation indicates a man with a firm grip on his household and a clear sense of his duty. Joshua as the successor to Moses in leading Israel is the true heir of Moses.

> Now fear the LORD and serve him with all faithfulness. Throw away the gods your ancestors worshiped beyond the River Euphrates and in Egypt and serve the LORD. But if serving the LORD seems undesirable to you, then choose for yourselves this day whom you will serve, whether the gods your ancestors served beyond the Euphrates, or the gods of the Amorites, in whose land you are living. But as for me and my household, we will serve the LORD.' (Jos. 24:14–15)

The Book of Judges

The book of Judges begins with a beautiful picture of fatherhood in the life of Caleb, Joshua's fellow faithful spy. Here is a father, who allows his daughters to have space to flourish as human beings. The picture is beautiful, carefree, and hopeful.[10]

---

9 Ellen Davis, *Getting Involved with God: Rediscovering the Old Testament*, (Cowley: Cambridge: Massachusetts, 2001), p.141.
10 Jdg. 1:12–15.

Yet the Book of Judges goes on to paint patterns of human sinfulness on a large canvas. It depicts a culture reaching the brink of moral collapse again and again. The main story of father and son is that of Gideon and his son Abimelek. This tragic story shows how this son kills his seventy brothers to become the king of his people, a role that his father had refused to accept even though the people had insisted. This treacherous murder is described as 'wickedness that Abimelek had done his father by murdering his seventy brothers' (Jdg. 9:56).

Is this whole sorry episode in part a failure of fatherhood? The seventy sons were born from Gideon's wives; Abimelek was borne by his concubine (Jdg. 8:31). Doubts about his legitimacy led the seventy sons to attempt to pay him off with seventy shekels of silver. The plan backfires as Abimelek uses the money to hire scoundrels who do the work of hired assassins. Fathers give a lead in life: when no lead is given the result is chaos.

At the centre of the book is the story of the penultimate judge Jephthah, whose tragic life highlights the different ways in which fatherlessness can play out in a person's life. Judges 10 – 11 record something of the impact of fatherlessness on a person and their family.[11]

Prophets, priests, and kings

The books of Samuel and Kings tell the story of the beginnings of Israel as a nation ruled by kings. It begins with the dark story of the spiritual blindness of the nation's religious leaders and the impact that has on national and family life. Eli, the High Priest, is presented as someone who is both slow to grasp what God is saying and doing, and one who has lost his grip on his sons, who run riot and bring disgrace upon him and his office. Samuel, Eli's young apprentice, is a spiritual giant by

---

[11] We will be looking in a subsequent chapter at an extended case study of fatherhood in the life of Jephthah, a man who provides a fascinating lens through which to view the dysfunctional nature of fatherhood.

comparison but like Eli he has sons who kick over the traces of their father's faithful leadership.

Throughout the books of Kings and Chronicles, kings are assessed in relation to the character and behaviour of their fathers. Tragically, usually when the narrative uses the expression of 'like father like son', it turns out to be very bad news indeed. Generally, the line of succession contains, with a few notable exceptions, many weak links. The sons struggle to rule justly because they lack any meaningful steering or example from their fathers.

King Saul and King David

Saul and David stand at the head of a line of kings of Israel and Judah, who as we have seen feature fathers who failed to prepare their sons for their roles as king, men and fathers. It is interesting to observe Saul and David and their experience of fatherhood.

King Saul appears to use his daughter Michal as a pawn in his mind games with David, his son-in-law and his rival for the people's affections. King Saul also very nearly engineers the premature death of his son Jonathan. In a story recorded in 1 Samuel, Jonathan undertakes a daring two-man raid on the enemy that results in a significant victory that sends the enemy into disarray. Saul had bound his people with an oath not to eat before the evening of that day. Any infringement of this oath will be met with death.

> But Jonathan had not heard that his father had bound the people with the oath, so he reached out the end of the staff that was in his hand and dipped it into the honeycomb. He raised his hand to his mouth, and his eyes brightened. (1 Sam. 14:27)

Part of Jonathan's celebration of victory was enjoying some honey he and his shield-bearer had found. The description of the reviving effects of the honey after an exhausting day are so vivid. Yet, trapped by his ill-considered vow, King Saul was all but ready to kill his son and would have done so, but for an uprising amongst his men. Saul as a father was paranoid, unpredictable, controlling, and abusive. His final action is to draw his son into a suicide pact to avoid being captured by the enemy. David's response to their death is to lament the loss of King Saul and his dead friend Jonathan. At the heart of the tragedy was a failure to be a father to his son and his nation.

> "How the mighty have fallen in battle!
> Jonathan lies slain on your heights." (2 Sam.1:25)

David

One of the rituals shared with my son as he was growing up was taking twenty minutes at 6 p.m. Monday to Friday to watch an episode of *The Simpsons*. This is a fascinating show that for 36 seasons has kept its finger on the pulse of contemporary life. Homer Simpson is possibly one of the most disastrous fathers of all time. In one episode he names his first two children and then in a moment of characteristic absent-mindedness refers to the third child as 'the other one'!

David was the eighth son of Jesse. Seven was the number of perfection so David was either a bonus or an afterthought. The latter seems the most likely because on the biggest day of his family history, a secret visit by Samuel the prophet to anoint one of Jesse's sons as King of Israel, David is not even invited. He had been sent out of town to look after the sheep. I guess David is a typical example of the slighted son.

David is a close friend of Jonathan, whose father King Saul, displays psychopathic tendencies. Saul is David's boss and then his father-in-law. David soothes Saul's troubled mind with his skill as a musician but when the catchy tune 'Saul has slain his thousands and David his tens of thousands' (1 Sam. 18:7) hits the number 1 spot in the charts, David is rewarded with Saul's javelin hurtling towards him.

You would think that given David's experience of fathers he would have been conscious of the need to up his own game in the fatherhood department. Tragically this was not the case. David's family life was like one car crash after another. David's record as a father includes: an illegitimate son who dies[12]; a son who follows his father's footsteps into sexual excess; a son who openly rebels in a daring military coup that places a ticking time bomb under David's reign and credibility; and one son who seeks to engineer royal succession in his own favour while David is on his deathbed.

At times reading these stories of Old Testament fathers feels like we are sitting in a rowing boat bailing out the water with a teaspoon, only to find that someone else in the boat is pouring it back in with a bucket. Here is a snapshot of part of the family:

> In the eighteenth year of the reign of Jeroboam son of Nebat, Abijah became king of Judah, and he reigned in Jerusalem three years. His mother's name was Maakah daughter of Abishalom. He committed all the sins his father had done before him; his heart was not fully devoted to the LORD his God, as the heart of David his forefather had been. Nevertheless, for David's sake the LORD his God gave him a lamp in Jerusalem by raising up a son to succeed him and by making Jerusalem strong. For David had done what was right in the eyes of the LORD and had not failed to keep any of the LORD's commands all the days of his life – except in the case of Uriah the Hittite. There was war between Abijah and Jeroboam throughout Abijah's lifetime. As for the other events of Abijah's reign, and all he did, are they not written in the book of the annals of the kings of Judah? There was war between Abijah and Jeroboam. And Abijah

---

12 When David marries Bathsheba, their son turns out by God's grace to be David's successor, but Solomon was a mixture of teacher of wisdom and man of folly, whose own extended family unravelled after his death.

rested with his ancestors and was buried in the City of David. And Asa his son succeeded him as king. (1 Kgs. 15:1–8)

Perhaps the darkest moment in this sorry history is the tragic story of a good king's bad son. Hezekiah is a bright spot in this narrative but his son Manasseh, who reigned for 55 years, did not follow in his ways; grace does not automatically run in the blood. Manasseh plumbed new lows in terms of fatherhood with the adoption of the pagan ritual of child sacrifice, causing his own son to pass through the fire (2 Kgs. 21:1–18). Yet astonishingly, it is recorded that Manasseh at the end his long reign humbled himself before God and removed all the idols from God's temple, although it did not permanently remove the attachment to idols in the people's hearts (2 Chr. 33:12–16). Manasseh's repentance provides a hint of hope for godly parents who for years have despaired of their children's behaviour and prayed and longed for their children to turn back to Christ. Maybe yet our sowing in tears will lead to us reaping with joy.

Spiritual Health Warning

Yet there is a warning here. Manasseh turned to the LORD, but the people did not. John Calvin described the human heart as a 'perpetual factory of idols.'[13] Idolatry is as invasive as bindweed or Japanese knotweed. Once it takes root it is a monumental task to get rid of it. Idolatry receives more attention in the Old Testament than almost any other subject; it could be

---

13 Calvin in the *Institutes* extensively explores this thinking. He describes human minds being like a 'labyrinth' from which speculative idols emerge. '...scarcely a single person has ever been found who did not fashion for himself an idol or specter in the place of God.' He adds that: 'just as waters boil up from a vast, full spring, so does an immense crowd of gods flow forth from the human mind...' John Calvin, *Institutes of the Christian Religion* ed. John T. McNeill, trans. Ford Lewis Battles (The Westminster Press: Philadelphia, 1960), 1:5:12 p108. See also: Book 1, Chapter 11, Section 8

argued that it is the issue that most often challenged the spiritual health of Israel. Idolatry is essentially the subplot of the Bible. No wonder one of the Ten Commandments spoken by the LORD via Moses states:

> 'You shall not make for yourself an image in the form of anything in heaven above or on the earth beneath or in the waters below. You shall not bow down to them or worship them; for I, the LORD your God, am a jealous God, punishing the children for the sin of the parents to the third and fourth generation of those who hate me, but showing love to a thousand generations of those who love me and keep my commandments.' (Ex. 20:4-6; Dt. 5:8-9)

The sins of the fathers do have a direct or indirect ongoing impact on children, and this impact might continue for generations, through lives blighted by the mess they might still need to be cleaning up. Yet it is worth noticing that Moses talks about this impact up to the third or fourth generation but also of the experience of love being shown to a 'thousand generations'.

I often find that discussions about this text get stuck in questions about the former while underplaying what is said in the latter. God interrupts the judgement with punctuations of merciful love, and the love outlasts the judgement. The negative aspects of idolatry will be felt by subsequent generations but the promise of love to a thousand generations points to an astonishing abundance of God's favour upon the fathers, children, and grandchildren of those who 'turned to God from idols to serve the living and true God.' (1 The. 1:9)

Arrows of Hope

One arrow of hope comes with the story of Manasseh's grandson, Josiah. His story is told in 2 Kings 22 - 23 and 2 Chronicles 34 - 35. Josiah was a fatherless son; his father's two-year reign was characterised by a departure from God's ways and came to a dramatic end when he was violently killed.[14] When Josiah was eight years old, he was thrust into the role of being king. You would think that with that start in life he would be a disaster like his father. Yet through wise mentors and the rediscovery of God's word, Josiah's heart was changed, and this change had a dramatic spiritual impact on the nation. I find this story so encouraging. It does not matter how disastrous a start you have in life; God can turn it around. In life, even for the fatherless, it can be darkest before the dawn. Like Josiah, I can be different to the bad example I had. The God of the Bible is the God who breaks through the darkest of stories.

I want to close this chapter on a further note of hope by reflecting on the final words of the last writing prophet in the Old Testament:

> "See, I will send the prophet Elijah to you before that great and dreadful day of the LORD comes. He will turn the hearts of the parents [fathers] to their children, and the hearts of the children to their parents [fathers]; or else I will come and strike the land with total destruction." (Mal 4:5-6)

Those words rang through the prophetic void for 400 years (before Christ). It is clear that the the issue of restoration is close to God's heart.

This urgent message concerns a promised realignment of relationships between fathers and children. This message is underlined in the angelic message given to Zechariah, the father of John the Baptist, when his birth is being announced (Lk. 1:17). This suggests that in the event of the coming of Jesus a work of reconciliation will be established that has an impact on every aspect of human relationships. This is an arrow of hope for all generations, especially a fatherless generation.

Questions

1) Although there are hardly any clear role models for fathers in the Old Testament, we do have some wise father to son wisdom offered in

---

14 2 Kgs. 21:19-26.

Proverbs chapters 1 – 9. Why do you think that such wise words often appear to fall on deaf ears?

2) We are used to the phrase 'like father like son'. How has what you have read in this chapter exercised you, and in what ways has it given you fresh hope?

Prayer

Heavenly Father, we praise you that in a world with so few good role models of fatherhood that you do provide some for us. Thank you for biological, surrogate, and spiritual fathers who have helped to support us and guide us in our lives.

We pray that you will help us to care for and support children of all ages, especially those who for one reason or another are fatherless.

Father of the fatherless, fill our hearts with your tenderness so that we can be agents of hope and change in our fractured society. In Jesus' name. Amen

Action

Think of your main takeaway from this chapter? Reflect on how it could inform your prayers and actions?

Complete the sentence: 'If there was one thing I could do to tackle fatherlessness, it would be—?'

'Where do I fit in in a world where I have got no father but I long for that? Where do I fit it in a world where I am not black, and I am not white?

He is going to teach me to be a man ... but he was not there.

I would idolize my dad because he wasn't there. It was easy to picture him as a superhero to me; he is going to take me to the park to feed the ducks! He's going to give me all his time and all his knowledge; and he never did. So, it was very confusing at times.

I knew that Jamaica was very Christian so I would say the Lord's prayer before I went to bed. I am not Christian, but I thought that saying the prayer would make me closer to my father.

That desire turns into anger, insecurity, and tears. Why am I not good enough? Why doesn't he want to take me out? Why doesn't he send me a birthday card on my birthday?' (Conor Allen[1])

'Sometimes I feel that my whole life has been one big rejection.' (Marilyn Monroe)

'Rejection is the constant theme in my life. If it were not for someone saying: I don't want you, there would be times when no one would be speaking to me at all.' (Cary Grant)

'It is the biggest problem we have in housing schemes and council estates and just in general. You see the impact of fatherlessness on a daily basis, in terms of people, young men in particular, getting involved in gangs, stealing, drugs, violence, not knowing how to control their tempers, attacking police and other organisations.' (Andy Constable, 20schemes, in conversation)

---

1 Connor Allen, Children's Laureate Wales 2021– 2023, in conversation.

Chapter 3 ~ Interviews: Repairing the broken picture ~ Different backgrounds, same wounds

It can be easy to think that people in the past were nothing like us, that we have come a long way since way back then. Yet studying them as we have just done actually highlights how little people have changed. We have different things, and wear different clothes, but our hearts are just as sinful and we are just as prone to make wrong decisions and behave badly. The interviews in this book with our contemporaries will show this honestly and clearly.

Fatherlessness in contemporary society can be an issue in any kind of family. It is not confined to certain ethnic groups or a particular financial status. It is also true to say that although it may happen in families of all kinds of backgrounds, the hurts and consequences can be very similar, if not the same.

Tony Sewell, CEO of the charity Generating Genius, writes about the controversy caused by the suggestion that many black boys are disadvantaged by their family background.

> Rod Liddle was branded a 'national disgrace' when he wrote about how black boys are paying the price for growing up in households without their dads. But he's right. The disproportionate number of black boys held in youth offending centres, which I visited during my time as a member of the youth justice board, shocked me.

Many of those I encountered had been involved in knife crime. So, what was going wrong? I did what many sociologists have failed to do: I asked them. These boys knew I wouldn't stand for any spin about racism or the closure of the local youth club. Without such excuses, nearly all pointed to the absence of their fathers as a key problem in their lives. It was straightforward: for these boys, the restraints were off, and they were simply left to fend for themselves.

Another interesting factor was the lack of responsibility these boys had for their crimes. All of them maintained that they were innocent. This 'not me guv' attitude even came from those who were caught red-handed with a knife. There is evidence to show that black boys are more likely to plead not guilty to crimes than their white counterparts. Inevitably, this leads to longer sentences when they are found guilty.[2]

The findings of the 2021 Census for England and Wales includes the following concerning lone parents: 85.9% of lone parents were female and 14.1% were male, like 2011 (85.6% female and 14.4% male).[3] It has become a cliché that many young black men grow up without a father. The statistics reveal that there is substance to the claim. Addressing the issue of the ethnic make-up of lone parents, the report says that those who identified as 'Black, Black British, Black Welsh, Caribbean or African: Caribbean' had the highest proportion of lone parents (51.0% compared with 48.5% in 2011). But people of every ethnicity can be damaged in some way by their father's absence. When this happens is it possible for that person to be mended?

---

2 https://www.spectator.co.uk/article/rod-liddle-is-right-about-black-boys-and-absent-dads/ accessed 09/01/2025

3 https://www.ons.gov.uk/peoplepopulationandcommunity/birthsdeathsandmarriages/families/articles/familiesinenglandandwales/census2021 accessed 09/01/2025

Stormzy, one of Britain's most successful Grime artists, spoke to a national newspaper about how he is learning to tackle his resentment towards his father who had left his family to start another one. Stormzy related that when he rose to fame, his father came back into his life to ask for money to buy a car. Speaking to *The Sun* newspaper, Stormzy said: 'It's very right that I hold this pain because of what he's done, with him not being there. Hes a flawed man, his mistake was a big one, but I know he's really sorry and he's reached out through my mother and my sisters. 'I am going to speak to him — I now have the power to say, "I forgive you".'

The rapper said he was willing to forgive him for abandoning his family. He sings in the song 'Please' from the 2022 album *This is What I Mean*:

> Please Lord give me the strength to forgive my dad because he is flawed and so am I, so who I am to not ... to not forgive a man who tries.
>
> I see his soul, I know it cries ...

In a BBC interview with Louis Theroux, he explains the background of the song. His Dad had asked for money to buy a car. In an earlier song, he had written:

> This pain is mine and I have the right to hold the pain in my heart.

When recording the new song, he found that he didn't feel like that anymore. Stormzy recognised that his father was a flawed man: 'I needed to give him the grace that I need.'[4]

The damaging effects of being fatherless are seen in attitudes, behaviour, and feelings of resentment, bitterness, hurt and anger. Although these things can take a long time to heal and change, as

---

4 https://www.bbc.co.uk/iplayer/episode/m001djpl/louis-theroux-interviews-series-1-1-stormzy accessed 09/01/2025

Christians we know that God provides the strength and power for such healing and change to happen. Let us start with interviews I conducted with two people with non-English heritage, one man and one woman who were willing to share something of their story.

Interview One, with a man:

- **What is the first thing that comes into your mind when you hear the word 'father'?**

I think in terms of my heavenly father now, but when I became a Christian, I struggled with the Lord's Prayer. When I heard 'Our Father', those words did not have very much resonance with me because of my experience or non-experience with my earthly father. I only saw my mother and father in the same room together when I was in my 40s. I only really came to terms with the word 'father' as a Christian.

- **Can you tell me about your father?**

After becoming a Christian, I wrestled with the fifth commandment: Honour your father and mother.[5] My Mum has always been around, and I love her, but with my father it is different. I remember when I was 20, I was walking through a park in London late one night. I had an overwhelming urge to know about my background. I wrote to my mother a painful letter that precipitated a journey into some kind of clarity. Up to that point I could count the times I had seen my father on one hand. I wanted to know stuff about how I came into being. The kind of things you tend to pick up when you grow up with them. Stories about how your parents met and so on. But I had none of that. From the age of 7 until I went to university I lived with my mum and grandmother. She put me in touch with him and

---

5 This is an important matter. I reflect more fully on the issues related to the fifth commandment for those who have negative experiences of parenthood in the free companion resource, available to download from https://www.gracepublications.co.uk/good-bad-no-dad-resources

we had a phone conversation, but nothing really happened as a result of that call. Then I decided that if I were to get married, I would invite him to my wedding. In part seeking to work out what the fifth commandment might mean in that situation. I invited him to my wedding, and I remember that two weeks before the wedding I had not heard whether he was coming or not. I invited him and my three half-sisters and they did not turn up.

A year later I contacted him and asked why he had not come to my wedding and there was no reply. Then I spent a decade abroad serving in a church, and when I came back, again I tried to contact him. My mum and dad were in touch with each other all this time. In the last ten years I have spoken to him more than in the previous forty-plus years of my life. It is still not quite what I would like it to be. I have a reminder on my phone to call my dad once a month. That is about it. Sometimes when I am in the area where he lives, I might pop in to see him. He often promises to come to see me, but he never has. My kids don't know him anywhere near as well as they know my in-laws.

- Do you ever think of how your biological father might have contributed to shaping you as a person?

Yes. Whatever way I look at it, he is connected to me in a way that no other man on this planet is. I was curious to know what he looked like, how tall he was, and his mannerisms. I wanted to know if he had any health issues. There has been a desire to connect to this individual who has got this biological link with me.

- How would you describe the fatherhood deficit that you have felt in your life?

I remember a quote from 2Pac, the rapper, who said he would have had more confidence as a man if he had a father in his life. He said that it teaches a man to be a man. I think there is some truth in that. I do feel like I am drawn to strong male personalities. I have worried over the years that I wouldn't have been as good a husband or father as I should be. On a positive note: I think the grace of God in the gospel has gone some way of making up for that deficit. My father has fathered eight children by five different women; someone noted that I had been the husband of one wife and had had four children with one woman. It is the grace of God that enabled that. I was 18 when the Lord found me, so I didn't have too much time to make major mistakes in my life. I received a good grounding in a good church that helped me to see how to live faithfully; that has gone some way to making up for the deficit left by the absence of my father as a role model.

- What have been the things that have helped you develop as a person who is fatherless?

I remember that my dad was two-timing my mum and one of my half-sisters was born in the same year I was born. He ended up marrying the other woman – I think I was an 'accident'. I therefore find Ephesians 1 quite comforting, that I was chosen before the foundation of the world. I wasn't an accident in God's eyes. When I became a Christian, I was mentored by a wonderful Christian man. He took me under his wing and took an interest in me as a man like no one else. Reading good Christian books shaped how I thought about who I was as a person. My pastor in my first church gave me opportunities to serve. It has been interesting that those who have contributed to shaping me have been white men! Although the person who led me to Christ was a black guy in his early 20s.

- Without an obvious blueprint for being a father how have you approached being a father?

I love my wife very much and am loved back. Our children were born out of the love I had for her and the love she had for me, so they were very much welcomed. I always wanted three kids, so our fourth was a bonus!

I remember a quote from Rico Tice, about an Olympic diver who had won a gold medal. He was asked how he could perform so well at such high standards. He said that: I get up onto the diving board, and I remember that my Mum loves me, and I just dive. He also said that whether he came first or last in the competition his mother still loved him. That for me was a picture of God's grace. That has been so transformative in my life. That is what I wanted to share with my kids. I remember saying to my kids when they were younger: 'You did so well; but you know that even if you didn't do well, even if you came last, daddy would still really love you.' We might not approve of everything they ever said or did, but we loved them. We had one rule: Honouring God meant obeying mummy and daddy without challenge, without excuse, and without delay.

- If you could communicate one thing about what it feels like to be fatherless, what would it be?

I think that one of the reasons that God gives us earthly parents is to teach us obedience to authority. So that ultimately, we can transfer our obedience from our parents towards God. If you are a good father, you can train your kids to realise that they need to submit to God's authority in their lives. I often imagine myself saying to my kids: 'It is not so hard to believe that there is a man in heaven, interceding and praying for you when you have a man on earth who prays for you.' Parenting your children well sets them up to know and love Jesus.

- How have you found your experiences have helped you in speaking to others who have had a similar experience?

I can relate to people in these situations. The fact that I grew up on a council estate without a father helps me connect me with other people who have a similar experience. It also reminds me that I am not the only one.

I am always drawn to and moved by depictions of relationships between fathers and sons. It reminds of the resentment; there is no getting back the years. Now I realise that my father was just a flawed man.

✳ ✳ ✳

It is interesting that flawed is also the word that Stormzy used about his father. It has become clear to me in the process of talking to people that men and women might experience fatherlessness in different ways.

Interview Two, with a woman.[6]

- **What is the first thing that comes into your mind when you hear the word 'father'?**

Father was not a positive term for me. Father meant rejection and failure. Failure on both sides. Failure of my father to be there but also failure in the sense of never being good enough. For the father's love and attention, you had to work.

A provider, to a certain extent, but it came at a cost. Father was not a word that I owned because I have three fathers. None of whom made me feel that I was an important or essential part of their lives. Betrayal is a word I associate with the word 'father' because in later life I realised that stories I had been told were lies. So, hearing about this Almighty Father was a real challenge for me. I could not relate to that at all.

My brother and I were adopted into a white family. We lived in a posh white area of London. My parents were very anti-religion. My mother was brought up Catholic and had rejected that. My father had attended a deeply religious school in Scotland and had been abused by one of the brothers who taught at the school. Then my parents divorced, and my mother got together with a man who was Jewish. Religion was a real no-no in my house apart from Hannukah. So, my brother and I started to attend a local Baptist Church by ourselves. We were too young to cross the busy road alone, so a Baptist church member would cross the road to get us to church. We started going because we were lost, and we were seeking something. The church and its members were beautifully welcoming to us. I turned my back on the church because I didn't really understand the

---

6 Second interview conducted on Zoom 17th August 2023.

message. Eventually I moved near to the South Coast and began to attend an Alpha Course and began to hear about Christ. It clicked when a person in the church was talking to me about how God loved me as a Father. I had to say: 'I don't get this. Father isn't good to me and every time you say that word it puts a barrier up.' Then the person said: 'Well you need to think of God as the father that you have always wanted and always needed.' That was a game changer for me!

- Some say that what is broken and missing about us because we do not know our fathers doesn't entirely get fixed and replaced. How would you describe the fatherhood deficit that you have felt in your life?

The fatherhood deficit is a huge one. You look to every other relationship to replace that deficit. Which means that you are looking for love in all the wrong places. You want a demonstrative display of love from someone, so you tend to look for the extremes. My first relationship was with a man who was an alcoholic, who was incredibly violent but when they said they cared about me they were demonstrative. I needed that real display, so I was searching for someone who said they cared and then you would accept all the awful things with it. The deficit was that I only knew about unhealthy relationships. I only knew about relationships where you chased affection and sacrificed your own feelings and never expected to feel whole. I expected disappointment, abandonment, failure, and rejection because that was the model I knew.

- Without an obvious blueprint for being a father how have you approached forming other relationships?

Without a blueprint it has been very bad. I have been in a lot of failed relationships. I have four children by four different fathers. There was an expectation that we were never really a family unit. I didn't expect that family unit to survive. Marriage was not an essential part of that either. When I became a Christian, I found myself ending the relationship I was in because I knew it wasn't good enough. It wasn't built on the foundation it should be built on, it was built on need rather than on mutual love and commitment. For the last season of my life, I have decided that it is best to remain single. Dating is not a healthy thing for me unless it is built on a Christian foundation.

With bringing up my children it has been very difficult. My two youngest children call me: 'Ma Dad', because they have not known their fathers and I have had to meet both those needs. It has been hard for my boys. My third son has not had a male presence in his life. There was a lot of anger, aggression, and confusion in him. He felt a sense of rejection down to his core. He struggles with his identity; he feels the need to prove himself as a man but didn't know how to. Instead, he has collected the negative traits of masculinity.

- Do you ever think of how your biological father might have contributed to shaping you as a person?

Yes, I do. He had quite a big impact. I got to meet him. He is dead now, but I was with him when he died. I told everyone when I was growing up that I was the love child of Diana Ross and Lionel Ritchie but that they had had me adopted because they didn't want me growing up in the limelight. I had these dreams that I had parents who loved and wanted me. I had information from social workers when I was young that my biological father did not want me adopted. When I met him, it was very emotional; he referred to me as his 'lost child.' So suddenly these feelings of being wanted and important to someone began to change the way I thought about myself. This became tainted after meeting him on several occasions, he sat me down and told me that he could not make the connection between the baby that was given away and the woman she has become. My own biological father said: 'I am really attracted to you, and I'd like to be in a relationship with you.' As a result, I didn't see him for a long time. I couldn't bear it.

When I got a phone call telling me that he was dying, I felt that I could not leave this world without resolving the matter. I jumped on a train and arrived at his house filled with people, who were at his bedside praying as he was slipping in and out of a coma. I climbed up on the bed to stroke his head and said: 'It's ok I love you.' I forgave him. He was hanging on for me to arrive; when I said those words, he died. It was quite a beautiful thing at the time. I had discovered that he had accepted Christ just before getting ill.

Then I accessed my adoption file and that was one of the most heartbreaking days of my life because I read that my mother had got pregnant while in a children's home. She had three children by the age of 17. The firstborn, a boy, was not with my biological father, but he put his name on his birth certificate, but he did not put his name on mine. My mother was told she had to give up two of the three children or lose them all. My father had said: 'We want the boy; you can keep the girl.' That absolutely destroyed everything. Everything was built on a lie.

- **What strategies have helped you develop as a person who is fatherless?**

Independence. I learnt that I can't rely on anyone. I learnt that people who shouldn't let you down are going to let you down. No one is going to be there for you in the end. I was very self-destructive, so I had to learn to like myself. That was one of the keys for me because if three different fathers do not like me and are not prepared to fight for me and put me first, I had to learn to do that myself. That was very hard. Your first instinct is not to like yourself because there is something unlovable about you. I was perplexed when people told me that the Father has forgiven me. My own father has not forgiven me or accepted me so how can this incredible being love me and forgive me? I have a biological father, an adopted father, and a step-adopted father. My adopted father has very high standards. He is a brilliant man but not the most empathic of individuals. You had to earn his love and respect. Someone telling me that God has given his love freely was a foreign concept to me.

- **How did you learn to receive God's love?**

It was very difficult. It was what held me back. It was having to step away from my experience of a father. It was having to separate that experience and saying: 'God is what I want as a Father not what I got as a father.'

- **Do you think there is an awareness of this issue in the church, and how important it is?**

No. That is why there are so many young people, especially those of colour, who have a second or third generation experience of fatherlessness. So, when people talk about God the Father loving us, they are not speaking into these children's lives, because they have no concept of this love. We do not need to change the message, but we do need to change the language we are using to a language they can understand. We are talking to young people who have no concept of a paternal lead in their lives.

- **How can Christians speak to this group?**

You must acknowledge the pain of their personal experience. Then you offer them salvation from the God who does not fail them as their fathers did. We need to acknowledge that some people have never experienced the loving arms of their father around them; they have only ever experienced the violence. They might have only experienced the anger and felt like a pawn in the game of their parent's relationship. You must speak truth into their lives. People need to be told that they cannot say that they do not need a father in their lives, because it is a lie. We need to remind them that the only father who will love them in this world is our Heavenly Father.

- What kind of relational superstructure can the church put into place to help fatherless people?

There are mentoring programmes like the Big Brothers Big Sisters programme where the church can make a difference.[7] These young people have not had a positive male role model speaking positives into their lives. There is a need to learn life skills like how to do a tie or have a shave, or how to respectfully address women. It is all well and good having preaching on a Sunday but there is the rest of the week when there is a need for truth to be spoken into lives. There needs to be some structure of one-to-one mentoring spending time each week sharing biblical wisdom and life skills.

There is a lot of invisibility in the Southeast. My town is a beautiful place, yet we have pockets of great deprivation, but it is hidden. We need to shine a light on it, acknowledging it without normalising it.

Inviting young people into our houses is very good but hosts need to be ready for the fact that this will open wounds. It is wonderful to be embraced in this environment but that you must go back to your own and then the pain kicks in.

- If you could say one thing to prepare your younger self for life, what would it be?

You need to find healthy love. Don't ever settle for second best or what is good in parts. Respect yourself and that will transfer into other relationships. Respect yourself in the way that God respects you and the way that Jesus respects all the women that he met. The world tells you to be in a relationship on any terms, grab what you want. Only when you let God speak into your life you will realise that there is a love that is right. Don't chase a love that is wrong for the sake of not wanting to be alone.

The pain I have gone through has put me in a unique position. So now I can work with people who are disenfranchised, rejected, and hurt by

---

7 https://www.bigbrothersbigsistersuk.org

society. God has used the pain in my life. I still have hurt in my heart, but I compare it to the absolute mind-blowing love when you connect with God.

***

Just as fatherlessness is experienced in all ethnicities, so it is across all levels of prosperity. Former Archbishop of Canterbury Justin Welby discovered at 60 years old that the man he called father was not his biological father. His mother had a brief relationship with Sir Winston Churchill's last private secretary Sir Anthony Montague Brown just before her marriage to Gavin Welby. Justin Welby discovered that he was the product of that brief encounter. Such stories could be replicated many times, as they have been in many historical novels.

Alongside these fractured stories of the socially privileged there are by contrast many more stories of the impact of fatherlessness amongst the working class. In a recently published history of the first century of the Labour Party I was interested to read that three of the founding fathers of the Labour movement were illegitimate at birth; this included the first Labour Prime Minister Ramsay Macdonald and the iconic (James) Keir Hardie, born of a mother who was herself illegitimate and after whom the current Labour Leader and Prime Minister Sir Keir Starmer is named. Combined with a truncated formal education this difficult beginning in life proved to be both a stigma and a stimulus. These men were never going to comfortably fit into society but this background became one of the catalysts for them to seek justice and fairness in society. The following story highlights the way that fatherlessness can both mar and make a person.[8]

The 2023 ITV series *Archie* tells the story of the Hollywood actor Cary Grant, who was born Archibald Leach in Bristol in 1904. Archie's early life witnessed some extreme poverty, the death of his older brother and the poor mental health of his mother. His father was often absent and

---

8 John Cruddas, *A Century of Labour* (Polity: London, 2024) p39, 50.

was abusive when present. Eventually his father committed his mother to a mental institution, later telling Archie that she had died (in 1936 he discovered that his mother was still alive and rescued her). One feature picked up in a review in the *Guardian* was his attitude to food:

> I think he was hungry for most of his early life. He was obsessive about not wasting food. If he saw someone throw something away, a half-eaten peach, he would grab it from the trash can and say, 'That's unkind.'[9]

I can relate to that. I remember not having enough to eat as a child. It can create anxiety about eating and obsessiveness about waste. For me, clean plates after a meal are a virtue; food left over is a vice!

Archie joined a travelling vaudeville troupe, and while touring in the US decided to stay and pursue a career there. He created a handsome relaxed debonair style of acting, that, with his mid-Atlantic accent resonated with cinema audiences on both sides of the Atlantic. As Cary Grant, he went through five marriages and several affairs, seeming to be unable to sustain deep, meaningful long-term relationships.

Grant also seemed to be reluctant to become a father himself, but did have one child, Jennifer, a daughter with his fourth wife Dyan Cannon. At the birth of Jennifer, he took the unprecedented step of stepping back from his acting career at 62 years old so that he could dedicate his life to being a father. It seems that becoming a father finally broke the emotional dam that had prevented him from receiving and giving love.

I was also interested to have a conversation with Andy Constable from 20schemes in Scotland about their preaching in a predominantly deprived working class area where fatherlessness is prevalent. Fatherlessness is the elephant in the room – the big problem that no one is talking about. Yet in some communities the issue is multi-

---

9 https://www.theguardian.com/tv-and-radio/2023/nov/13/cary-grants-hollywoods-archibald-leach-mother-archie accessed 18/12/2024

generational, with some families having no clear blueprint of fatherhood in living memory.

Interview Three

The following interview was planned as a wide-ranging interview about fatherlessness in the UK but took an unexpected turn when the interviewee began to talk about her own experience.[10] This has been a common experience in the interview sections of this book. I anticipated going in one direction, but the interview has often then gone off in another direction entirely.

- What are the major causes of fatherlessness in the UK?

I want to go with sin. Growing up we are not taught life skills. So all the things we need to know in adulthood (and the more deprived an area we grew up in the more true this is), you are not taught anything to do with leadership, in terms of how to lead your own life or how to lead your family. I can't remember a single thing about this. There is also a lack of mentors. You must get onto some kind of list or some degree of trouble before you get one.

We are not taught a lot about emotional and mental well-being even though these are seen now to be very important. Where do we get help if we want to understand why we react in the way that you react in certain circumstances? I think it comes down to education, by which I mean how we educate and lead each other.

- What is the first thing you think of when you hear the word 'father'?

When I became a Christian, I swore that I would never call God 'Father'. This was because of my own experience of being fathered. My own dad was abusive and serially unfaithful to my mum with a multitude of women. We could have gone on the Jeremy Kyle Show with various kids coming out

---

10 Interview conducted 8th June 2023.

of the woodwork and DNA tests and all the rest of it. Various people did emerge from time to time and say to my dad: 'I think I am your daughter.' Eventually my parents split up when I was 16, and it was the best thing that could have happened to me. My siblings did not experience it in the same way. I had been a Christian for a year at that point; it felt that it was a gift from God, which I was not sure that I was allowed to say. Because of the way that divorce is spoken of in church I would have been very cautious about who I said it to in church back then. It felt like such a huge relief.

I do now call God 'Father'. One of the greatest joys of my Christian life has been discovering God as my Father. But I have had to work really hard to deliberately push into what is it to call God Father when you haven't got an idea of what fathering actually is. I can call God Father, because it is a word; but it doesn't mean anything. At one point I asked God to reveal to me what fathering means. Ten years ago, I wrote a list about what it means to correct, direct and be tender-hearted in discipline, to dote on and to champion and to cherish. All these different words came to mind. I realise that I had begun to call God Father but do not know what it means. God revealed himself to me as Father through men in the church.

The first person who was a father figure to me was the man who led me to Jesus. He was a teacher in my school. Although I would not have realised or articulated it, I was definitely learning about fatherhood through him. He is probably only just about old enough to be my dad if he had been a teenage dad. I guess that at that point I started to be fathered and it was in my relationship with him that I started to see God as Father, but it was through the lens of this guy. Ten years ago, it turned out that he had been in a pretty spectacular moral failure for a couple of years. His whole family imploded, and I had a bit of a crisis of faith. I worked for the church so I could not really have a crisis of faith; I could internally but I couldn't externally. It was not hidden; the church leadership here knew about it. I remember going to this man who led me to Jesus and looking him in the eyes and asking him who he is. Are you the man that I have known as a father-figure or are you an abuser? Are you like my own dad, basically? That was a crisis. I think the truth is that he was used by God to reveal some aspects of the fatherhood of God to me, but he was more like my earthly dad than I knew. Partly it was the shock of it. With my own dad I have never known anything different. But with this man's failure I felt that the foundations of my faith had been illegitimated.

Since then, I have done a lot of hard work with God to make sure I look at God directly as father, and not through the lens of someone else. At the same time as that I would say that God has placed amazing men in my life. My church leader here, who definitely is not old enough to be my dad, has been like a steady older brother. It has been wonderful to serve under strong godly men; there has been no drama. In the last two years I have known a very deep joy in knowing God as Father. It is not dependent on these men in my life. If all these men fell, now what I have got with God is much more between me and him. So, I would be devastated but I do not think it would rock my faith in the way that it did with the first guy.

- **Do you think that the church gets how big a deal fatherlessness is?**
No. It is weird because it is a thing that we talk about now and then.

We need to be reminded that fathers are a gift to us, and they are supposed to point us toward God. When they do not do this, it is devastating. It is like putting on sunglasses; everything is suddenly darker. Poor fathering or absent fathers are similar, we are seeing everything through a filter. Imagine some guy comes up to me and says: 'I have heard about your relationship with your dad and wondered if I could come alongside as a father figure.' Probably I am going to go: 'creepy!'

- **The gospel does address these things about our father deficit, but it does not make you any less fatherless. Have you found that a challenge?**
Yes. I have had counselling from a professional counsellor, who is also a Christian.

I found that to be tremendously helpful, even to think about how the pathways of your brain are formed. Why I am more likely to react in a particular way, but also equipped to deal with these triggers? There is perhaps a fear of talking in church about things that might be regarded as psychobabble. I have found that God has used these professional skills to really help me develop my own self-awareness. I think the church doesn't really get the impact of it. I don't think that we realise that so many ways that we interact are because we have been triggered by something. Six years of counselling has helped me to completely change the way I relate to people. I feel pretty steady and stable myself. Not everyone in the church has the confidence to see that the transformation of the gospel can change the way we think and behave so that the person we become is not the person we were.

What I found most difficult when I became a Christian and over the years, I have met lots of people who have had great relationships with their dad. Even now I struggle to know whether what they are talking about is ok. Sometimes seeing a woman my sort of age interacting with her dad can be really upsetting for me. It is more likely to trigger me than seeing someone mistreating their daughter.

- Do you recognise any contribution your biological dad has made to the person you are?

Yes. Resilience. There is a tenacity I have. My deep-rooted desire for justice comes from my dad. Not in a good way. I remember as a ten-year-old sitting in my lounge with a deep sense of rage, because it all seemed to be so unfair and I was powerless to do anything about it.

That has translated into a commitment I now have to justice issues and powerlessness. I don't think I have ever got so far as thanking God for the dad I have had. But I do thank God that he has used the experiences to shape who I am.

My verse for the day on a Bible App was 'Honour your father and mother.' I was utterly shocked and kind of annoyed that the guy in the *video at no point referred to the fact that people might not have had a brilliant model of mothering or fathering. It was almost as if he assumed that everyone had a perfect dad. It depends on what your situation is with your dad. My dad is alive, and he is local. From time to time he is in my life and at other times not in my life. Mostly this is based on whether he feels like it or not. So, it is not a done and dusted issue. I think that in church the way mother and father relationships affect us is little understood.*

- **What about Father's Day?**

I usually will not go to my own church on Father's Day. I don't know why it matters whether I am in my own church or not.

- **If you were framing a series of sermons on the fatherhood of God and fatherlessness, what would you want to be saying?**

I would want to see an acknowledgement of the seriousness of the lack of fathering or bad fathering. Present but not good. One of the reasons I find Father's Day painful in church is because we honour all the dads in the room as if they are all equally good. I would want to hear dads being called to be good fathers. I would want to hear men in the room, single, married divorced being asked 'Who are you fathering and are you doing it well?'

What does it look like to be doing it well and if you are not doing it well, there is a need to repent and offer the hope of change? If you regularly raise your voice, if you use unkind words, what damage might this do? Some really practical examples of what good and bad fathering looks like and how dads can change.

✳ ✳ ✳

For those who experience fatherlessness, whatever their background, there are many common issues that have to be processed: Feeling something is missing in your life and identity; a curiosity about a biological father; a resentment towards them; feeling rejected and a failure; looking for love that can be relied upon. These are some of the many father issues that can mar and make us.

We began this chapter with Stormzy, singing about his desire to use his pain to paint a broken picture, to turn it into something that is better despite being made up of broken, painful parts. That is an incredible image: is it possible that the story of the broken pictures of fatherless relationships can be fixed? Can we bring our lives and our society to God's repair shop and fix what is broken?

Thankfully, people can make progress coming to terms with fatherlessness, even if they always walk with a limp. Our interviewees talk about breaking the cycle of fatherlessness in their families so that they can build a better future. For this to happen people need to hear the call to embrace responsible parenting. This is a call for people of every nationality to step up to the plate and be the mothers and fathers that a growing child needs to grow up in a safe and happy environment. The church has a unique role in this process. We have the biblical message that sets a high bar for the integrity of parents, we can provide good role models of what it means to be a father and point people to the grace of God in Christ that introduces people to the perfect father by the power of the Spirit. Things that are broken can be mended. Ugly lives can be beautified. The wounded can be healed. Those stuck in the narrative of fatherlessness can find a new script for their lives. One of the distinctive things about the gospel is that it brings hope, where previously there was none.

The consequences of fatherlessness identified by our interviewees included the issue of trust and the relationship with a stepfather or other father figure.

Men seeking to fill the place of an absent father as a mentor or stepfather need to make an honest and realistic assessment of what is possible and desirable in their relationship with another person's child. Aspiring father figures need to be careful to avoid Messiah Syndrome in their approach to the vulnerable; such an approach can be oppressive and controlling, and potentially do more harm than good. As with all acts of service, those who reach out to help need to make sure that their aim in seeking to help a person is to serve the Lord and the person faithfully and sensitively. For vulnerable people there might be the need to overcome an unwillingness to trust others and let them into their lives. 'Once bitten twice shy' we say, but we do need to be open to being loved. As CS Lewis so aptly put it:

> To love at all is to be vulnerable. Love anything and your heart will be wrung and possibly broken. If you want to make sure of keeping it intact you must give it to no one, not even an animal. Wrap it carefully round with hobbies and little luxuries; avoid all entanglements. Lock it up safe in the casket or coffin of your selfishness. But in that casket, safe, dark, motionless, airless, it will change. It will not be broken; it will become unbreakable, impenetrable, irredeemable. To love is to be vulnerable.[11]

Learning to trust someone to enter our lives can be one of the most massive steps we can take. At times we cannot be 100% sure whether this will be traumatic or transformative. While a person will want to make all the checks and balances, we must acknowledge that there are no risk-free relationships. Trust is not a blind leap of faith, but it does require us to take a step of faith.

> One who has unreliable friends soon comes to ruin,
> but there is a friend who sticks closer than a brother. (Pr. 18:24)

I remember Tim Keller once saying: 'A friend is someone who lets you in but never lets you down.' If you want to be a blessing as a father figure, be that friend. If you want the blessing of receiving father-like care, learn to find ways to trust.

---

11 C. S Lewis, *The Four Loves*, (London: HarperCollins, 1999), p.77.

Questions

1) What in this chapter has made you think differently about the fatherless? What difference might that make to your attitudes and prayers?

2) How does a person identify the emotions, attitudes and actions in their lives that are shaped by their background?

3) How can fatherless people begin to see God as the father that they have always wanted and always needed?

Prayer

Father God. How difficult yet how delightful that name is to me.
Heal the wounds of fatherlessness in me. Grant me the healthy sense of significance and security that flows from me being your child.
I pray for those who struggle with a sense of rejection, that you would help them to know your restoring grace and reassuring presence.
I pray for all those who struggle with their identity, who are puzzled by their origins, and wounded by a father deficit; Father God lead them to the father they have always wanted and always needed.
I pray for those who are seeking to deal with less than ideal father figures, biological, step and spiritual.
I pray that those who take the role of father figures for the fatherless will be wise and sensitive in the way that they initiate and develop relationships. I pray for the ability to learn how to build trust and to show trust in these situations.
Father God, thank you that when I come to you, I know that I will never be short-changed, disappointed, or abandoned.
Thank you that in coming to you I encounter a Father, whose fatherly care is rooted in eternity and will hold me throughout my days and forevermore.
In Jesus' name. Amen.

Action

If you have any responsibility in a local church, think of ways that you can provide informed teaching, robust support structures and sensitive role models for those who have no one on earth that they can call father.

Do some research on work amongst the fatherless. Think about how you could be more informed and involved.

Here is one place to start: https://safefamilies.uk

'I have no blueprint for being a father.' (Mark Strong)

'The biblical stories function as a mirror today of something true about human experience, both the ancient world and the twenty-first century. They can be horrifying and depressing. People dominate, hurt, and abuse each other, both then and now. The stories also show people being courageous and graceful and resisting evil.' (Lynn Japinga)

'In this story, bad parenting, bad religion, and bad judgement, come together in a perfect storm of violence.' (David Marcus)

'We cannot tolerate the silencing of memory, lest it happen again. '(Elie Wiesel)

Chapter 4 ~ Case Study: Judges 11 - 12 Jephthah

> What he did (the sacrifice of his daughter) is a thing that all Scripture condemns; why he did it (to keep his word) is a thing all Scripture commends.
>
> (Michael Wilcock)

Modern biographies often spend time on three things: beginnings, endings, and the achievements in between. This chapter will look at the beginning, middle and ending of Jephthah's story. When we look at the bookends of Jephthah's life, we see two aspects of fatherlessness etched into one life.

Beginnings

> Jephthah the Gileadite was a mighty warrior. His father was Gilead; his mother was a prostitute. (Jdg. 11:1)

What an opening line for anybody's story. Jephthah is a man of status but with an inconvenient twist. Jephthah was a somebody, who was never able to entirely wrestle free from being a nobody. Jephthah is the illegitimate son of a local landowner; the story of his origins sounds like something out of a Victorian novel.

The introduction to this story has real shock value. Jephthah's parentage is a study in contrasts, he is a somebody because of his distinguished father, but he is a nobody because his mother is a prostitute. This inauspicious start planted a seed of rejection in Jephthah's heart: rejected by his father and his biological father's family. Rejection stings and stains. Is there an emotional wound here that does not heal? We are often defined by our origins. They leave a mark on us that time often fails to heal. Donald Miller writes that:

> Not everybody who grew up without a father lacks confidence and emotional health, but the connection between the two is undeniable.[1]

Pastoral Reflection

When I recently spoke about Jephthah to a group of students in Latvia there were nods of recognition from many in the room. Latvia is a matriarchal society with a history of absent or passive fathers, therefore I should not have been surprised by what happened next. The preaching seminar was on pause for a few minutes as one after another spoke of how this story resonated with their own. We heard stories of fathers who had left the family home and the impact this has upon those left behind. Questions rise in the minds of children: 'Why did my Dad leave me?' 'Did Dad stop loving me?' 'Did I do something wrong?' 'Who will be my Dad now?' Fatherless children are always looking for the security that the presence of a father is supposed to represent. Many of the examples given in this book are of men but there are many women who have spoken to me about the gaping hole that fatherlessness has left in their lives. Some people try to laugh it off with their talk of 'Daddy

---

1 Donald Miller, *Father Fiction: Chapters for a Fatherless Generation*, (Howard Books: Brentwood, 2019), p.11.

issues', some people can't talk about it at all, and live behind a smoke screen of 'coping'. The sense of abandonment and vulnerability resulting from fatherlessness leave emotional scars and psychological wounds that do not heal easily.

This is a live contemporary issue that is more widespread than most people imagine, as JKA Smith puts it:

> LATE CAPITALISM is the age in which everyone has a computer in their pocket and a gaping hole where their father should be.[2]

Unfortunately, as with most holes in our lives, we try to fill the vacuum with anything, but nothing quite fits the bill; or we try to pretend that there is no hole there at all.

In his book *How to Inhabit Time*, Smith shows remarkable vulnerability as he talks about his own experience of his father leaving his mother, resulting in his mother, Smith and his siblings having to leave the family home. Later, when married and a father himself, his family moved to a new house and Smith realised that it became a trigger that brought back his childhood memories of the divorce and leaving his own family home as a boy. I talked to Smith about this in an interview for *Inspire Magazine*. I asked about exploring our vulnerabilities and Smith replied:

> What I realised was that I had in a sense buried traumas, experiences from the past that were banging on the basement door of my life and manifesting in problematic ways. The only way to tame those monsters was to go into the basement.[3]

One of the things I would like this book to accomplish is to create a safe environment where people can be honest and vulnerable about how they feel and seek help in exploring how to deal with them. Perhaps

---

[2] James K A Smith, *On the Road with Augustine: A Real World Spirituality for Restless Hearts*, (Brazos: Grand Rapids, 2019), p.195.

[3] Interview conducted by the author for *Inspire Magazine Online*.

hearing echoes of their own stories in those of other people will act as an arrow of hope that points to the reality that they are not the only ones who have experienced this.

The things in-between

How are we to view Jephthah? Mary Evans makes the following positive assessment:

> The narrative as a whole makes it clear that he was a gifted man, perhaps the most gifted of all the leaders/deliverers described in Judges. Not only was he a good fighter, an able military commander and a strategic thinker, he was also a diplomat.[4]

Taking a more negative view, Timothy Keller suggests that: 'Jephthah was in organised crime; a kind of underworld boss, or (more romantically) a pirate. He was a complete outcast and a criminal from a broken home.'[5]

Jephthah is a man of status but with an inconvenient paradox. He is an insider and outsider at the same time, he is a complex character who does not appear to be completely at ease with himself.

The name Jephthah means 'he opens'. This accurately describes his career, in which he acts like a can-opener to prise open opportunities to progress in life and prevail in battle. Jephthah comes over as a man who does not take 'no' for an answer and will eventually wear down any opposition with the force of his persistence. Jephthah is like a dog with a bone. Has Jephthah's personality got anything to do with his beginnings? Is there an element of insecurity, an inferiority complex that somehow he needs to mask by bravado? Some fatherless sons do this by becoming the life and soul of the party, feeling that they must always make people laugh. Others do so by trying to be the smartest,

---

4 Mary Evans, *Judges and Ruth: Tyndale Old Testament Commentaries*, (IVP: Leicester, 2017), Kindle location 2268.
5 Tim Keller, *Judges*, (The Good Book Company: London), p.113.

bravest, richest, or most dominant figure. Did Jephthah have a sense that he needed to compensate for his unsatisfactory beginnings? Some people feel that they need to work twice as hard to get half as far. Could Jephthah be one of those individuals who simply tried too hard?

There is a sign early on in the Jephthah story that indicates that he felt the need to demonstrate his credibility by going beyond what was necessary. For example, when he had received the unconditional offer of leadership of the men of Gilead, he feels that he needs to make a solid offer more solid.

> Jephthah answered, "Suppose you take me back to fight the Ammonites and the LORD gives them to me – will I really be your head?"
>
> The elders of Gilead replied, "The LORD is our witness; we will certainly do as you say." (Jdg. 11:9-10)

Pastoral Reflection

Being fatherless, like having any deficit in our lives, can lead to a person growing up with a chip on their shoulder. When you feel that you have not made the grade or that you do not fit in, it can have a dramatic psychological impact on a person. Some of the ways that this can manifest include trying too hard to impress, being overly defensive, and taking rejection badly. It is a great gift and a blessing to live at ease with yourself, not always feeling that you have something to prove. When we feel that every word we speak and every action we perform needs to be justified, we become prisoners to our insecurities.

This attitude of insecurity can blight anybody's life, but it is particularly devastating in the life of a leader. There can be value in becoming what Henri Nouwen describes as a wounded healer. Aware of our vulnerabilities we can lead with understanding, sensitivity, and tenderness. By contrast insecure leaders can speak and act out of their hidden wounds, their strong leadership being a mask to hide their vulnerabilities. Tragically the outcome, as we will see in this story, is that such leaders begin to inflict crushing wounds on others.

The Ending

Turning now to the moment when Jephthah finally opens his mouth to utter his controversial vow. We have seen how Jephthah has the tendency to go beyond what God has required. Is that what is happening here? What is clear is that Jephthah's actions are a chilling narrative of the failure of fatherhood. He makes his rash vow without thinking through the consequences. It is ironic that part of Jephthah's early success concerned his way with words in negotiating his role with the elders and in his wise diplomacy with the Ammonites. Such care with words escapes him at this moment.

Again, it is ironic that the vow was not necessary in the first place. No one was asking him to make a vow; it is an example of him going over the top. His words to God in verse 30, 'If you give', may show some insecurity in his own position but certainly show an incorrect view of God, querying God's ability to keep his promise.

Did he know that it was an Israelite custom for young women coming out to greet the victorious in battle? Did he fail to anticipate this or did Jephthah want victory more than anything else in the world, whatever the cost?

The innocent girl, unaware of her father's rash vow, does what young girls often do when their dads come home: rush out to greet them. That is often one of the nicest parts of returning from a long trip away.

The tragedy unfolds with the further irony of Jephthah's response to his daughter's carefree celebration of his safe return. He blames his daughter for how he is feeling, thus displaying a complete lack of emotional intelligence.

When he saw her, he tore his clothes and cried, "Oh no, my daughter! You have brought me down and I am devastated. I have made a vow to the LORD that I cannot break." (Jdg. 11:35)[6]

When wounded insecure people strike out in self-justification, they tend to disregard the feelings of others. Jephthah was supposed to protect his only child, a virgin daughter, who was vulnerable. Instead he exposed her to the tragic consequences of his actions. In some ways there is a reversal of roles at the end of this story. The father who should be bending over backwards to protect his daughter finds himself comforted by her. This is a contrast to Jephthah's lack of sensitivity toward his daughter's pain. Nobly his daughter seeks to see the situation from her father's viewpoint and is willing to pay the cost of sharing her father's pain.

Jephthah's daughter remains nameless, anonymous and helpless. Her father does not appear to do anything to mitigate the consequences of his rash vow. The nameless daughter's first words are 'My father'; almost her last words, 'my friends' (11:37). It was her friends who provided the comfort that her own father seems to be incapable of offering. Jephthah had not experienced the love of a father and he seems unable to offer it. His cruel start in life had made him hard as nails, self-sufficient and emotionally deficient.

The story of Jephthah and his daughter calls to mind the story of Abraham and his son, Isaac, an only child who Abraham is told to take as an offering. The most obvious parallel between the Jephthah story and Genesis 22 is that in both stories fathers are prepared to sacrifice their children, literally or figuratively. But there are significant differences. In

---

6 Lev. 27:1-8 suggests that there was a way out of an ill-advised vow and elsewhere human sacrifice is forbidden (Lev. 18:21, 20: 2-5; Dt. 12:31; 18:10). There is of course no sign in the story that Jephthah was aware of such teaching. This was the time of the Judges, when chaos and muddle tended to muffle the claims of truth.

Genesis 22, it is God who proposes the test; here Jephthah proposes the test – it is not required by God.

Barry Webb helpfully sums up Jephthah's life.

> Jephthah is a capable man – capable with words, capable in battle; he has a strong, decisive personality and is a leader of men. At his best he can exercise exemplary faith. But he has a background, a personal history, which helps us to understand his limitations even if we cannot condone them. He is insecure and self-centred. He can never fully engage with anyone's interests but his own. This is the hardness in the man and the reason that he can never be truly great. It is to this insecurity and self-interest that his daughter is sacrificed. Jephthah cannot be a father.[7]

Pastoral Reflection

- **Gifts and Grace**

The Spirit appears in the story to equip Jephthah for battle, (Jdg. 11:29), but being enabled by the Spirit to do a job does not guarantee moral transformation in a person (see the warnings of Jesus in Mt. 7:21–23).

- **The Sound of Silence**

God's response to Jephthah's vow and its devastating outcome is silence. Christine Redwood writes:

> God does not make Jephthah say his vow, but neither does God stop it. In this story when human beings choose destructive decisions, Yahweh does not intervene. The people of God are also silent; nobody objects.
>
> It is God, or God's absence, that makes the story so problematic.[8]

---

7 Barry G Webb, *The Book of Judges* (TNICOT), (Eerdmans: Grand Rapids, 2012), p.343.
8 Christine Redwood, 'Preaching Old Testament Narrative to Australians (69-86)' in Ian Hussey (ed), *Preaching with an Accent: Biblical Genres for Australian Congregations*, (Morling Press, 2019), p.74.

God offers no comment on the vow or its consequences. What are we to make of this story?

As we have seen, Old Testament narrators do not tend to offer opinions about the actions of their character. Jephthah is not condemned in the text, he is listed with Gideon, Barak, and Samuel as one of Israel's saviours (1 Sam. 12:11). He also gets his name in lights in Faith's Hall of Fame (Heb. 11:32). John Thompson makes use of a commentary by the Puritan Richard Rodgers,

> who looks forward to Hebrews 11:34 and proclaims that the praise in that verse for those "who by faith grew strong" surely applies to Jephthah's daughter. In effect, this Puritan preacher has given Jephthah's daughter the place on that roll of heroes that she had previously been long denied. Rogers goes on to tell his flock that the annual lament described the end of Judges 11 as a fitting custom – and "It should not be forgotten."[9]

Judges 11:40 indicates that there was an annual commemoration of the daughter of Jephthah the Gileadite. But what happened to her? The jury is out on that one. There is no dead body in the text. Some writers like Phyllis Trible take the worst-case scenario, seeing this incident as one of the texts of terror, that relate how badly women were treated in biblical history.[10] Others want to argue for her being spared from death but having a life restricted to a nun-like vow of celibacy. In favour of her being sacrificed is her own emphatic statement that her father should do what he had vowed: 'Do to me just as you promised' (Jdg. 11:36), and the statement in verse 39 that 'he did to her as he had vowed.' In favour

---

9 John L Thompson, *Reading the Bible with the Dead: What can you learn from the history of exegesis that you can't learn from exegesis alone?*, (Eerdmans: Grand Rapids, 2007), p.44.
   Richard Rogers, *A Commentary on Judges*, (Banner of Truth: Edinburgh,1983), p.584.
10 Phyllis Trible, *Texts of Terror*, (Fortress Press: Minneapolis 1982).

of something else, like her being a 'perpetual virgin', sacrificing her freedom, is the double reference to the fact that she would not marry and the additional statement that she was a virgin.

Whatever action was taken after Jephthah's rash vow meant that his daughter lost her 'life'. It didn't have to end like this. Jephthah's reign is the shortest of all the judges, just six years, and he has no descendants (Jdg. 12:7). His epitaph could be 'successful in battle, failed at life!' For us it might be 'successful at the office, factory, shop, church, but failed at life.'

What Jephthah's daughter needed from him was for him to be a father. When the crunch came Jephthah was missing from his post and his daughter feels the sting of fatherlessness in its many forms.

Questions

1) Do you hear any echoes of this story in your own life or the lives of people you know?

2) Did you learn anything about how you could help yourself or others with the issues explored here? Could we help others see a clearer blueprint of fatherhood?

3) What could we do to honour the memory of Jephthah's daughter today?

Prayer

Father God, thank you for all of those who have had a great start in life. It is so easy to take this for granted and to look back at this story from a position of moral superiority. Humble us we pray. Forgive our foolish ways. Help us to see the wounds that life has inflicted on us and help us to seek your healing before we inflict wounds on others.
Guide our thoughts with your wisdom, form our words by your truth, and shape our lives by your grace.

We pray for those who have been wounded by the rash words and harsh actions of others.

We pray for those children who have looked for love and security in their fathers but have found neglect or cruelty in their place. Heal their wounds. Wipe away their tears. Grant them the tender embrace of your love. Break the cycle of toxicity. Help them to begin a new season in their experience.

In Jesus' name we pray. Amen.

Action

Use the following words from Ecclesiastes to make an inventory of your words and promises. Think about how you can take care to say what you mean and mean what you say.

> Guard your steps when you go to the house of God. Go near to listen rather than to offer the sacrifice of fools, who do not know that they do wrong.
>
> Do not be quick with your mouth, do not be hasty in your heart to utter anything before God. God is in heaven and you are on earth, so let your words be few.
>
> A dream comes when there are many cares, and many words mark the speech of a fool.
>
> When you make a vow to God, do not delay to fulfill it. He has no pleasure in fools; fulfill your vow. It is better not to make a vow than to make one and not fulfill it. (Ecc. 5:1-5)

Learn to rejoice with those who rejoice and weep with those who weep. The Book of Judges could be called The Book of Weeping – 2:4; 20:23, 26; 21:2. There are so many chaotic and broken things in these stories that are a mirror of so much that is out of place in our times. How might the biblical concept of lament help us to identify with those who mourn what has been snatched from their lives?

'I had two fathers: a public one and a private one.
    I loved and admired my public father. He was a respected university professor with a strong work ethic. He was willing to pay the steep tuition costs for all six of his children to attend a Lutheran elementary school. On Sundays, he made sure we were all neatly lined up in church at the front of the sanctuary. Dad was ambitious, intelligent, and charming.
    My private father was a completely different man. At home he frequently went into rages that terrorised the entire family: shouting, punching, and kicking. He would call us pigs and stupid idiots. He was quite open about his violence, saying, "Do this or I'll beat you." Then he carried through on his threats. His favourite tactic was the knuckle fist—the knuckle of the middle finger slightly extended to create a sharper stab of pain as he punched us. He was careful to hit us where the bruises would be covered by our clothing, so that no one at school or church ever suspected. Watching my siblings get beaten was as traumatic as experiencing it myself.' (Nancy Pearcy)

'Why is the pain of every day translated so constantly into our dreams, in the ever-repeated scene of the unlistened-to-story?' (Primo Levi)

'While I pray, O Lord, help me to be open to every grace from above and sensitive to every need around me. Train me in ways of loving that will bring justice and healing to others, even as you direct me by your Holy Spirit. Amen' (Eugene Peterson)

Chapter 5 ~ Interview: Mending the broken hallelujah ~ Child abuse

Following our look at some of the so-called Texts of Terror in the Old Testament I wanted to include a section on child abuse. In previous generations this subject was surrounded in a blanket of silence but now has come front and centre in public awareness. This is the #MeToo generation that has learned that it is possible to blow the whistle on abusers and be heard. High profile cases like those of the celebrities Rolf Harris, Gary Glitter and Jimmy Saville, and church abuse scandals worldwide have made it more difficult for people to hide from the damage caused by those who abuse children. The Irish novelist John Boyne, famous for his children's novel *The Boy in the Striped Pyjamas*, turns something of his own experience of being abused into the novel *A History of Loneliness*. The book captures with devastating clarity the difference between a little boy before and after being abused by a priest. Ironically priests take the name Father, but the actions of some of them are a denial of any fatherly compassion or care.

> And then before I could turn away, Aidan came running out of the living room like Speedy Gonzales and threw himself into my arms so hard that he nearly knocked me over. 'Goodbye Uncle Odie,' he roared. 'Adios amigo!' 'Adios amigo!' I replied, laughing as I turned away, and when I reached the door of my car I looked back and

> there he was, standing in the doorway next to Tom, who had a hand on his shoulder, my nephew waving so hard that I thought his arm might fall off, the grin on his face threatening to split his face in two. And that was the last I ever saw of Aidan. Of that Aidan. The next time I was in their house, a week or two later, he was a different lad altogether.[1]

John Boyne communicates well the dark sense of loss that comes when the sunny optimism of a child is snatched away by an adult, who should make him feel safe, but instead introduces the dark threads of threat and danger. Some children never entirely recover from this abuse of trust. John Boyne describes what the victim continued to feel: 'The damage that man did to me in one night is damage that I will take to the grave with me.'[2]

Mez McConnell in his moving and harrowing memoir *The Creaking on the Stairs*, describes how difficult it is to try and deal with the ongoing consequences of abuse:

> For some the journey will be longer than for others. Sadly, far too many of us will sink into deep depression. We will self-harm, we will drink too much, hide in drugs, or move from one disposable relationship to another. I suspect that far too many of us have been on the road to self-loathing and self-destruction for far too long. Maybe you've grown tired of it. Maybe you've grown tired of life. Tired of waiting for answers that never come. Tired of crying in dark corners.[3]

Generally people talk about abusive fathers, and for good reason, yet, as Mez McConnell reminds us, women are also capable of physically,

---

1 John Boyne, *A History of Loneliness*, (Kindle Edition, 2024), p. 252.
2 John Boyne, *A History of Loneliness*, p.284.
3 Mez McConnell, *The Creaking on the Stairs: Finding Faith in God Through Childhood Abuse*, (Fearn: Christian Focus, 2019), p.35.

psychologically, and sexually abusing children. McConnell offers a pathway to peace, but it is not an easy one, for it travels through the challenging terrain of forgiveness, even for those who have hurt us.

I do book reviews for a few Christian publications, which means I get sent lots of books. Some of these books grab my attention instantly; others are ones that I would have chosen to have read anyway, so that is a bonus. We tend not to look at self-published books; there is often a good reason why a publisher has not chosen to publish a book. I made an exception when I was sent a book by Nel Bennet (not the author's real name) with the title A *Chance to be Sorry: Forgiving those who are not sorry*. The book is made up of two halves of uneven length. The first half, the longest section of the book, is a moving story well-told. I would guess that the author is of my generation, as I recognise many of the cultural references. It must have cost the author to tell this story, which contains a truck load of trauma in a tragic story of broken families, abuse, conflicted loyalties, and paralysing fears resulting from these experiences. The author paints the picture of her life without descending into sensationalism or bitterness. The story unfolds with an honesty about the pain but also leaves room for the cracks that allow the light to shine through. A major part of this light comes through her Christian faith and the support received from the church; this despite one church contributing to the problem. The story explores the need and desire for a sense of being heard and for justice to be done and seen to be done. I contacted the author to ask her a few questions about her story.

Interview Four

- You have experienced two fathers: your biological father who had severe mental health issues and your ex-stepfather who abused you. How would you describe them?

Describing my real Dad, who I lived with until I was seven years old, I would say that he was present, loving, and fun but unwell. On reflection he was more like another child, but he was present. My real Dad had custody of us; this was so usual in the 1960s. With my granny at his side, he was able to look after us. They were both unconventional. My father's moods were very up and down, he would either be full of generous spontaneity or sober. He had an absent father because his mother became pregnant by a man that she described as being 'out of her league'. She never revealed the man's identity to my father. He had a lot of bitterness about that, which was made worse when my mum went off with someone else. He had a breakdown when my mum began to get visitation rights. He didn't seem to be able to cope with her turning up with the man she had run off with. My mum took the opportunity of his breakdown to snatch us away. We have this memory of a fun dad, who was very loving and good with children and grandchildren.

Then my mum took us to this home with this great big man, over six-foot-tall and weighing over 20 stone. He was a very good provider and a hard worker. He seemed to be fine at first, but within a few weeks he began to be violent, and then after a few years sexually abusive. It is very confusing to have a stepfather like that who does a lot of good for his family, he was a better cook than my mother, he could do anything, he was clever and made things (I was very good at woodwork when I was at school). Yet he was a bully and an abuser. Describing my ex-stepfather who I lived with aged 7–17 years old, I would say that he was present but abusive. He was a good provider, but his abuse over-shadowed our lives then and now.

- **When you wrote *A Chance to be Sorry* – you said that you wanted to help others – what kind of feedback have you received?**

I gave a talk at a women's event before the book was published. I had always envisaged that I would go to small groups, but I ended up with a room full of 80 women. The feedback from that was affirming. So many women came up to me at the end and said: I have never told anyone about this, but this happened to me. It affirmed the estimates that one in seven people have had sexual abuse in their childhood. People who have read it have said that they found it helpful.

- **How therapeutic was it for you to write this book?**

It took me ages to write the book. I don't think that I set out to write a book. My husband bought me a journal when we had reported the perpetrator. We didn't tell many people, but others were aware that we were going through something. The more I journaled the more I realised that there was nothing out there that was helpful from a non-secular viewpoint. It was painful to write, but it has helped me to make sense of things and be more boundaried in terms of challenging what people say and what I won't challenge. I have become more self-aware through researching the subject and recounting my experience and my faith.

- **What are the ongoing wounds and scars of your experience?**

My health has taken a big knock. I have a sister, who went through similar experiences to mine. She always had really bad mental health. She has always expressed her pain but up until that point I had not expressed myself, because this space was taken by my sister. My body has said 'I can't cope with this.' I have fibromyalgia and other issues that link back to the traumas.

I feel the need to defend people who have gone through something similar, which can be exhausting.

- What goes on in the mind of a child/young person who is being abused – how did you cope with trying to be normal when things are not normal in your childhood experience?

It was learning to take the positive things and not letting the abuse steal that from me.

- How have your experiences shaped the way that you have approached your marriage and motherhood?

I have put myself under a lot of pressure to get it right. My children think that I was pretty relaxed, but I was always aware of what might go wrong. It has made me more aware, but I have tried not to be overprotective.

- Your story explores the need for being heard and for justice to be done and seen to be done. Why is that important and why is the process complicated in practice? Why is it important to keep forgiveness and justice together in your thinking?

When my mother knew about the abuse, which is when I was 16, I was told that I could not say anything about it. We did try to reach out to a few places for help. As a Christian we feel that we should be forgiving. I have found this message difficult because I have not been aware of how to do it. It was only after doing the Freedom in Christ Course that we went through the steps to freedom that I realised that there could be justice with mercy. I never wanted my stepfather to be harmed but I did want him to face justice. He was too old when the process began so he never did.

- How has this affected your attitude to God?

I always start my prayers with the words: 'Heavenly Father'. I was fortunate, I did have a good, albeit imperfect biological father in the first part of my life. That gave me a glimpse of what a father might be like. I had a glimpse of what a loving father could be, so when I faced a bullying, abusive stepfather I was able to challenge it in my mind: this is not the way it is supposed to be. I turned to God and the Bible, and this gave me my identity.

- **What would be your advice to your 12-year-old self?**

Run! We did try but we kept being brought back. Turn to God, try to get into a church and get as much support as you can. The trouble with running is that you lose all your family support. When we reported the crime, the wider family rejected us. With my mum I made up my mind to treat her as if she was a good mum. That was a forgiveness thing. That is what God does – he treats us well.

- **Do you experience those flashback moments and what triggers them?**

People's words. When I had my children, I realised my biological father did not do things for me but needed me to do things for him. We do have some good memories and I do identify with the 'Stockholm Syndrome' as, at the time, I felt protective towards the family unit, including him.

- **How can the Church be aware of the vulnerable?**

It can provide examples of hope. We had a really good Father's Day service a couple of years ago. We had a guy speak at the service about his own experience as a fatherless man who is now in a good family.

In the book Breakthrough by Giles Lascelle, the author talks about the church being trauma informed. I used to work in marketing and public relations, where there was always an emphasis on staff training, but what I realised was that people are put into roles, but they are not trained for them. The same can be the case in the church.

***

What can the church do?

Mez McConnel helpfully reminds us that this prevalent issue is often not discussed: 'Nobody talks about it and yet so many adults in my church and many more associated with it, have suffered physical and/or sexual abuse as children.'[4] McConnell offers the following reason for the silence and its consequences in the lives of those who have been abused:

> What makes the figures more frightening (and speaking from personal experience) is that the majority of child abuse incidents are never reported. This means that most of the people we come into contact within our daily lives have more than likely been abused in some form during their childhood and formative years. There is a lot of guilt and shame around the issue, which makes discipleship a slow process and that can take up an inordinate amount of time, and therefore requires a high commitment from those doing the discipling.[5]

There are three things that the church can do to address this issue.

Firstly, it can be a subject that is spoken about upfront in the church

I have been thinking about how that could be done using Psalm 10. Here is a Psalm for the wounded and demoralised. It talks about perpetrators, victims, and justice. Reading and preaching on psalms like Psalm 10 can help abuse victims see that they are not invisible and unheard but are taken seriously by the church and by God. The following meditation is an attempt to wrestle prayerfully with this Psalm that links abusive behaviour with fatherlessness.

Psalm 10

1 Why, LORD, do you stand far off?

---

4 Mez McConnell, *The Creaking on the Stairs: Finding Faith in God Through Childhood Abuse*, (Fearn: Christian Focus, 2019), p.184.
5 Mez McConnell, *The Creaking on the Stairs*, p.185.

Why do you hide yourself in times of trouble?
2 In his arrogance the wicked man hunts down the weak,
    who are caught in the schemes he devises.
3 He boasts about the cravings of his heart;
    he blesses the greedy and reviles the LORD.
4 In his pride the wicked man does not seek him;
    in all his thoughts there is no room for God.
5 His ways are always prosperous;
    your laws are rejected by him;
    he sneers at all his enemies.
6 He says to himself, "Nothing will ever shake me."
    He swears, "No one will ever do me harm."
7 His mouth is full of lies and threats;
    trouble and evil are under his tongue.
8 He lies in wait near the villages;
    from ambush he murders the innocent.
    His eyes watch in secret for his victims;
9   like a lion in cover he lies in wait.
    He lies in wait to catch the helpless;
        he catches the helpless and drags them off in his net.
10 His victims are crushed, they collapse;
    they fall under his strength.
11 He says to himself, "God will never notice;
    he covers his face and never sees."
12 Arise, LORD! Lift up your hand, O God.
    Do not forget the helpless.
13 Why does the wicked man revile God?
    Why does he say to himself,
    "He won't call me to account"?
14 But you, God, see the trouble of the afflicted;
    you consider their grief and take it in hand.
    The victims commit themselves to you;

> you are the helper of the fatherless.
> 15 Break the arm of the wicked man;
>   call the evildoer to account for his wickedness
>   that would not otherwise be found out.
> 16 The LORD is King for ever and ever;
>   the nations will perish from his land.
> 17 You, LORD, hear the desire of the afflicted;
>   you encourage them, and you listen to their cry,
> 18 defending the fatherless and the oppressed,
>   so that mere earthly mortals
>   will never again strike terror.

Psalm 10 is the second half of an acrostic poem that begins with Psalm 9. Together they follow the 22 letters of the Hebrew alphabet to trace out the need for justice. This is a creative way to communicate the comprehensive nature of the call for justice for the oppressed. Psalm 10 has two main sections and an epilogue.

Section One: The Abusers' Taunting (Ps. 10:1-10)

This part of the Psalm is a lament offered by the abused that begins in verse 1 with the question 'Why?' Why does it seem that God is absent without leave or looking the other way?

The abuser is depicted as a predator who hunts down the weak (2, 8-9). His heart is captivated by distorted desires and his mouth is full of boastful and evil speech (3). As Derek Kidner puts it: 'One of his chief weapons is his tongue, whose varied techniques of intimidation and confusion are suggested in the long catalogue of verse 7.'[6] He thinks that he is untouchable (6), that no one, not even God, sees what he is doing (11); everything is hidden in plain sight. Many abusers make use of the cover of darkness to preserve their dirty little secret.

---

6 Derek Kidner, *Psalms 1-72*, (IVP: Leicester, 1973) p.71.

This section also graphically describes the impact of all this on the victim: 'His victims are crushed, they collapse; they fall under his strength.' (10) The victims appear to be overwhelmed, helpless, and have nowhere to turn.

This could almost be describing the experience of an abused person who has been cowed by cruel words and dominated by a strong arm. One young man told me that when he and his brother had to move back in with his biological father as boys, the first thing his father had said to them was: 'Look at these hands.' Those boys had many reasons to be afraid of those hands before they eventually left home!

Section two: The victims' prayer (Ps. 10:11-15)

This section begins like verse 1 with a sense of frustration that God does not appear to be paying attention:

> He says to himself, 'God will never notice;
> he covers his face and never sees.' (11)

This is followed by the main petition on behalf of the helpless: 'Arise, LORD' – a cry that is an echo of Psalm 9 (9:19-20; 10:12). This was an ancient battle cry used by Israel when the ark was brought out to lead the army in battle against the enemies of the people. Here it is used as a prayer that God will intervene in this unjust world.

Ironically this prayer for the LORD to notice the sufferer is rooted in the assumed attentiveness of God. Prayer puts us in the presence of God, where we realise he is with us. He is not looking the other way – he is deeply and intimately interested in us! Verse 14 says, "But you, God, see the trouble of the afflicted; you consider their grief and take it in hand." The Psalmist is encouraged to know that the LORD has taken note of their trouble and grief.

It is at this point in the psalm that we see the connection with this book. The LORD is described as 'the helper and defender of the fatherless' (14, 18). Sometimes this word is translated as orphans but the connection between fatherlessness and abuse still stands. The psalms give us words we can use when we pray. For the afflicted it can be a great comfort to know that others have taken this path before, navigated it and found help.

Perhaps one of the biggest challenges for the fatherless and especially the abused is the sense of powerlessness they feel. The abuse involves being overpowered and the ongoing trauma can make the victim continue to feel that they are under the abuser's oppressive power. Therefore the requested intervention is 'Break the arm of the wicked man; call the evildoer to account for his wickedness that would not otherwise be found out.' (15) To break the arm is to break the power and so neutralise the force they want to use to crush us.

Eplilogue: The God who listens, encourages, defends and drives away fear (Ps. 10:16-18)
Seen through the lens of the gospel we can affirm that we have a king who gives us access to the throne of grace, where we can find mercy and grace to help in time of need (Heb. 4:16). A king who suffers with us and for us; he is the servant king who conquers through sacrifice. He knows the depths of our despair and can sound the depths of all our deepest concerns. He has brought us into a relationship with our Heavenly Father, whose perfect love drives out fear (1 Jn. 4:18).

Secondly, the church can provide a safe place for the abused to talk about their experience in a context where they will be heard and accepted
As this book was being prepared for publication the *Makin Report* was released on 7th November 2024. The findings of this report were based on an investigation into John Smyth, who was a key leader of the Iwerne Bible camps in the UK, and similar activities in Zimbabwe and South Africa. The report outlines Smyth's sexually abusive behaviour that involved more than 100 boys over four decades. Part of the fallout from this report has been the resignation of the Archbishop of Canterbury,

Justin Welby. This incident is a reminder that church and church based activities are not always safe places for vulnerable people. There needs to be a greater sense of humility shown by the church concerning the places where it has failed to be a safe place, and authentic and sustainable strategies to strengthen commitments to healthy safeguarding.

Cathy Newman of *Channel 4 News*, who had been instrumental in bringing the story to public attention interviewed Smyth's son PJ, who had also been a subject of sexual abuse by his father. The 25-minute interview was broadcast as the main item on *Channel 4 News*. The final part of the interview included this sad but illuminating exchange:

> Cathy Newman: It's just over a week ago, I think, that the *Makin Review* was published. 251 pages, a brutal exposé, really, of your dad's abuses in three different countries. What did you think when you read it?
>
> PJ Smyth: I think that it cemented my father as the most prolific abuser connected to the Church of England. And I think it cemented the Church of England as needing rapid and radical changes in terms of their response to abuse.
>
> Cathy Newman: What words, or word, would you use as his son to describe him?
>
> PJ Smyth: Grand narcissist, barbaric, even monstrous, and my father.[7]

Smyth's son's responses reveal the complex and conflicted emotions of a child who has been abused by their father. This mixture of fear, horror and revulsion is mixed with the remaining experience of connection with their fathers and control by them. It is this sense of

---

7 https://www.channel4.com/news/the-words-of-john-smyths-son-pj-one-of-his-earliest-victims-in-an-exclusive-interview-with-this-programme accessed 25th November 2024

never entirely being free of the shame that can continue to haunt a child, however old they are!

It is common for those who have suffered abuse, physical, psychological, sexual, or spiritual to breathe a sigh of relief when they finally find someone who will listen to them. Such a supportive listening environment can also provide a safe place where the abused can explore the impact of their experience on their lives. As we have observed, the experience of abuse can contribute to physical and mental illness; it can make a person less able to give and receive love; and it can make forming and maintaining close relationships difficult.

In some circumstances there are darker consequences of the experience of abuse. People who have been abused have spoken to me about the impact of abuse on their thought world and actions. Sometimes abuse can produce dark thoughts and dreams where the abused becomes the abuser. These thoughts and dreams are as unsought and unwelcome as they are disturbing. It can be puzzling and depressing for a person who has experienced the trauma of abuse to have such thoughts invade their imaginations.

Others have spoken to me about how being abused has created a pattern of thought and behaviour in their lives that it is difficult to escape. Child abuse is sometimes called ritual abuse because it can take place with the same person, in the same place and time each day or week, until it is established as normal behaviour. It is almost inevitable that such repeated 'rituals' will have an impact on the lens through which a person views human interaction. I have spoken to individuals who were abused as children, who have gone on to abuse their own children. I want to stress that this is not true in every case where a person has been abused but it is something that happens. This does not excuse the abused turned abuser, but it does provide a context for understanding the dynamics involved. This phenomenon is explored in a book on idolatry: *Bound to Sin, Abuse, Holocaust, and the Christian Doctrine of Sin* by Alistair McFayden.[8]

McFadyen's application of the concept of idolatry to the themes of sexual abuse is as stimulating as it is controversial. One very helpful insight is his unpacking of how idolatry in its concrete forms distorts the whole of life. McFadyen explores how being a victim of sexual abuse can so define and shape a person's identity and life direction that it becomes an idol to them, in the sense that it is the organising principle around which they live their lives. He writes, 'Not only does the idol override all other claims, it bends the whole of life into its exclusive service'[9] adding that, 'Idolatrous dynamics colonise the whole of our life intentionality as a false and falsifying dynamic supplants that of worship of the true God.'[10] McFayden concludes:

> Abuse easily insinuates itself into a child's total way of being, relating to, interpreting, and communicating in every context of interaction. It can distort the deepest structures of personhood and identity.[11]

McFayden writes that this results in the following four factors in a person's life:

- Traumatic sexualisation (By which he means that sexual experience has been awakened in a child both prematurely and in a context that is abusive and unhealthy. This can have a lasting and detrimental impact on a person's self-image and their ability to relate to others.)
- Betrayal

---

8 Alistair McFadyen, *Bound to Sin: Abuse, Holocaust, and the Christian Doctrine of Sin*, (Cambridge: Cambridge University Press, 2000).
9 Alistair McFadyen, *Bound to Sin*, p.225.
10 Alistair McFadyen, *Bound to Sin*, p.226.
11 Alistair McFadyen, *Bound to Sin*, p.73.

- Powerlessness
- Stigmatisation

Churches seeking to come alongside victims of abuse need to be aware of these issues, able to identify ongoing trauma related to them, and ready to offer support and counsel to begin to deal with some of the consequences.

Thirdly, the church can equip the abused with a theological framework
Those who have been abused may have a jumble of feelings that arise when thinking about their experience and the abuser. The complex web of memory, respect for the family, forgiveness and justice can be difficult to navigate. As Christians our beliefs and the language of our theology provide a frame that helps us cope with and understand our own lives and the wider world.

Christians have been freely forgiven and we are called to freely forgive. Yet it can be difficult to forgive those who have not owned up to the wrong they have done for us. The willingness of the abused to forgive the abuser releases the abused from the burden of being unforgiving. The weight of that burden can continue to wound the heart and make the abused person find it difficult to experience to the full the grace of God extended to them. Forgiveness is made easier – although it is still costly – when the abused acknowledges the wrong they have done and seeks forgiveness. Then there is the prospect of reconciliation, where two people are set free: the abused and the abuser.

The call to forgive those who have wronged us can seem like another attempt by the abuser to manipulate and control the abused. Yet forgiveness is complex and needs to be thought of hand in hand with justice. I might be willing to forgive someone who has wronged me but if that wrong involves something that needs to be put right, or breaking the law, it is also right for me to seek justice. This can bring some closure for the abused but also honours justice by calling the abuser to account and perhaps helping to prevent them from easily abusing again.

For some abused people, the idea of their abuser being forgiven seems like a bridge too far. This is something that Mez McConnell deals with at length.[12] In answer to the question, Can we both forgive our abuser and hope for them to be punished at the same time, McConnell replied:

> I hope so. That's how I felt for many years. My issue would be to ensure that a person was pursuing justice and not vengeance. Vengeance belongs to the LORD. But I have great respect for those who pursue their abusers and see them brought to justice. I sometimes still wonder if I should have pursued justice in my case.[13]

A Final Word: Hope

To suffer abuse as a child is an awful thing. Its consequences are devastating, complicated and challenging. The scars remain for a lifetime. Yet the abuse endured does not need to be the final chapter in their story.

I was moved to hear about the award in the New Year's Honours List of the British Empire Medal to the nine-year-old Tony Hudgell. Tony is the youngest recipient of such an honour. It was awarded for his efforts in raising £2 million for charity by completing several 10K walks and a 238-metre climb in the Lake District. This would be quite an achievement for any nine-year-old, but Tony is special. At six weeks old he was in hospital struggling for his life due to horrific abuse caused by his birth parents. Tony sustained multiple fractures, dislocations and

---

12 Mez McConnell, *The Creaking on the Stairs*, p.195-217.
13 Mez McConnell, *The Creaking on the Stairs*, p.217.

traumas that led to organ failure, toxic shock and sepsis. Doctors were left with no option but to amputate both his legs at the knee.

Tony's adopted parents have given him love and stability and encouraged a positive attitude to life. Tony, who says that he would love to climb Everest one day, has used his traumatic past to motivate himself to help other vulnerable children.[14]

Tony's story is a beautiful reminder that any story beginning with ugliness does not need to end that way. For the abused, we have seen and heard that there is hope to be found in God. For those in churches, we can pray for empathy and the love, kindness and wisdom necessary to care for those who have suffered in this way.

Questions

1) Both Mez McConnell and Nel Bennet (at the beginning of the chapter) tell their stories from the inside. For them abuse is not an academic subject, it is their experience. How does reading their stories help to think and pray about this matter?

2) If you have been a victim of abuse, how has this section of the book helped you to process what has happened to you? How might you use Psalm 10 to pray for yourself if you have experienced abuse?

3) If the contents of this chapter have been foreign to you: Praise God but do seek to be sensitised toward those who have suffered and learn to care for them.

Prayer

Father God, I praise you that I have been set free to use the name 'Father' for someone who loves me with an everlasting love, accepts me in the Son that he loves, and will never let me go.

---

14 www.thetimes.com/uk/article/my-son-is-the-youngest-honour-recipient-but-we-kept-it-a-secret-from-him-bw92205qp   accessed 17/12/2024

I pray for those who still feel very keenly the sting of abuse past and present.

I pray that they will experience the tenderness and restoring power of your fatherly love.

Break the power of those who have wounded them. Lead them to your restoring grace and peace. Guide them to understand that they may seek both to forgive and seek justice.

I pray for churches to see their blind spots in this area and learn to identify cases of abuse and deal with them with wisdom, transparency, love and courage.

Action

Think about ways that you could make your church more trauma informed.

Seek to support the place of safeguarding in your church; encourage your church leaders and safeguarding officers as they fulfil their duties in this. Safeguarding has many aspects including protecting and caring for the abused and working with abusers – work which will be largely confidential. Expressing your support without asking for detailed stories is a big encouragement!

Working with the abused and abusers is challenging and it would be wise to seek expert support from professionals. Do some research on the agencies and resources that can equip churches to handle vulnerable people with insight and compassion. For example: www.traumabreakthrough.org

'To trace the image of the father through the Bible is to see the general outlines of biblical theology in microcosm.' (Dictionary of Biblical Imagery)

'Against this backdrop of the failure of fathers stands the image of God the Father, who exemplifies all these characteristics that flesh-and-blood fathers lack: patience, kindness, firmness, attention.' (The Dictionary of Biblical Imagery)

'We do not truly understand God's work as Creator or his providence (and so have no comfort) unless we understand that it is a fatherly work.' (Michael Reeves)

'A father to the fatherless, a defender of widows,
is God in his holy dwelling.
God sets the lonely in families,
he leads out the prisoners with singing;
but the rebellious live in a sun-scorched land.'
(Psalm 68:5–6)

Chapter 6:
God the Father in the biblical story
~ Old Testament

After reading the stories of human fathers in the Old Testament it is a breath of fresh air to turn to the rare but beautiful pictures of God as Father that are recorded there. 'The litany of paternal failures serves as a reminder that only one father is good.'[1]

Yes, and how good he is. The picture of God as the ideal father is breathtaking.

People tend to think that the idea of God as Father is a New Testament idea, but as Jim Packer put it: 'Father ... is the Christian name for God.'[2] This, of course, is only partly true. It is certainly true that the full blaze of revelation concerning God as Father is found in the New Testament, but we miss many insights if we ignore the Old Testament witness.

The first man and the people of God

The concept of father and son is used in the Bible to describe the basis of two of the most foundational relationships between God and human beings, Adam, and the nation of Israel.

---

1 *Dictionary of Biblical Imagery*, p.274.
2 J.I. Packer, *Knowing God*, (Downers Grove, IL: InterVarsity, 1973/1993), p.201-202.

The first indirect reference to God as father is found in Genesis 1-3. The first man, Adam, is described by Luke in his genealogy of Jesus as the 'son of God' (Lk. 3:38). God is depicted as the perfect father who provides everything that is necessary for Adam's well-being. We can say confidently that the fatherly care of God was perfect. What did that look like? God the Father was present, accessible, and dependable. Even when God ejects Adam and Eve from the garden it is an act of gracious discipline that protects the couple.

The idea of God as 'father' and Israel as 'son' is decisively embedded in the Exodus narrative when making Israel his people. Then Moses is directed to say to Pharaoh,

> 'This is what the LORD says: Israel is my firstborn son, and I told you, "Let my son go, so that he may worship me." But you refused to let him go; so I will kill your firstborn son.' (Ex. 4:22-23).

This theme is echoed in Hosea 11:1, a verse that was later to be repurposed and fulfilled in the life of Jesus as he returns to Israel after his childhood exile in Egypt (Mt. 2:14-15). In bringing Israel out of Egypt and bringing them to the Promised Land, God is seen as a father-figure, caring for his people in every dimension of their lives. This is beautifully described by the Psalmist:

> As a father has compassion on his children, so the LORD has compassion on those who fear him; for he knows how we are formed, he remembers that we are dust. (Ps. 103:13-14.)

God the Father in Deuteronomy.

Perhaps one of the most important sources of reference to God as Father in the Old Testament is in the Book of Deuteronomy. Of the forty-one references to the fatherless in the Old Testament, eleven are found in Deuteronomy.[3] This makes it a significantly important theme in the book, as the final reference makes plain:

> "Cursed is anyone who withholds justice from the foreigner, the fatherless or the widow." Then all the people shall say, "Amen!" (Dt.27:19)

Deuteronomy contains four illuminating pictures which teach us precious characteristics of the fatherhood of God.

An image of touch: Carrier (Dt. 1:31)

> Then I said to you, "Do not be terrified; do not be afraid of them. The LORD your God, who is going before you, will fight for you, as he did for you in Egypt, before your very eyes, and in the wilderness. There you saw how the LORD your God carried you, as a father carries his son, all the way you went until you reached this place."
>
> In spite of this, you did not trust in the LORD your God, who went ahead of you on your journey, in fire by night and in a cloud by day, to search out places for you to camp and to show you the way you should go. (Dt 1:29–33)

God the Father describes himself as the one who has Israel's back, who fights for them and leads them safely by fire and cloud; something better than any Sat Nav. Yet it is the image of God as a carrier that highlights his main fatherly role here. Maybe that is where the anonymous author of the poem *Footprints* got the idea of being carried. I imagine a picture of a father carrying his child in a sling strapped around his chest; close enough for the toddler to hear its father's heartbeat and feel his reassuring breath. This intimate picture is echoed in the book of Isaiah, who speaks of God as a shepherd:

---

3 10:18; 14:29; 16: 11,14; 24:17,19,20,21; 26:12, 13; 27:19.

> He tends his flock like a shepherd:
>> He gathers the lambs in his arms
> and carries them close to his heart;
>> he gently leads those that have young. (Is. 40:11)
>
> God is seen as a Father-figure, caring for his people in every dimension of their lives.[4]

The fatherless long for a relationship like this. Some people have grown up without any personal attention from their fathers. They have never experienced being held close to their fathers; they have not been carried close to their father's chest. They have not been protected, delighted in, or given directions for life. Instead of being carried many of the fatherless feel that their 'dads' have dropped the ball, ignored, and abandoned them.

An image of meaningful interaction: Trainer (Dt. 8:5)

Children have a lot of growing up to do. They learn by looking and listening. Role models who provide an example of how to do life are invaluable. Fatherless children long for people who at different stages of their lives will tell them how to do this and that. That is what we have in this second image of God as teacher or trainer.

> Be careful to follow every command I am giving you today, so that you may live and increase and may enter and possess the land the LORD promised on oath to your ancestors. Remember how the LORD your God led you all the way in the wilderness these forty years, to humble and test you in order to know what was in your heart, whether or not you would keep his commands. He humbled you, causing you to hunger and then feeding you with manna, which neither you nor your ancestors had known, to teach you that man does not live on bread alone but on every word that

---

4 PC Craigie, *Deuteronomy*, (Eerdmans: Grand Rapids, 1976), p.380.

comes from the mouth of the LORD. Your clothes did not wear out and your feet did not swell during these forty years. **Know then in your heart that as a man disciplines his son, so the LORD your God disciplines you.** (Dt. 8:1-5, my emphasis)

All this talk of discipline can send a shiver down the spine of those who have had cruel and abusive fathers. Yet as Amy Peeler helpfully writes: 'Discipline need not be the same as abuse. In fact, at times, lack of discipline is evidence of abuse via neglect.'[5]

The setting of boundaries and understandable directions for taking the right path, and clearly defined sanctions for straying from the path are precious gifts from a good father. It is important to see that the biblical concept of discipline is primarily about training, not punishment. God the Father is committed to the development of his children, he is determined to enable them to make progress. It is interesting that verse 3 of this section is one of the three quotations from Deuteronomy that Jesus uses to answer Satan's temptations.[6] All three quotations are from the section in Deuteronomy 8 - 12 that unfolds the importance of trusting in the fatherly care of God and learning to walk in his ways.

The writer to the Hebrews picks up Deuteronomy 8:5 when he talks about God's love for his children.[7] God the Father loves us so much that he is not afraid to take us through difficult things in our lives to help us grow. When the writer to the Hebrews talks about the development of Jesus, he uses the daring phrase 'Son though he was, he learned obedience from what he suffered.' (Heb. 5:8)

Here we are standing on holy ground, but clearly our training to be God's sons and daughters will also involve a process that will not always be comfortable but will always be good.

---

5 Amy Peeler, *Women and the Gender of God*, (Eerdmans: Grand Rapids, 2022), p.222.
6 The other references are Dt. 6:16, 13.
7 Heb. 12:5-11 see also Pr. 3:11-12.

An image of delight: Favoured (Dt. 14:1)

One of the great surprises when first turning to the pages of Deuteronomy is how much of the love of God we find in its pages. The motivation for being a distinctive people is the growing realisation that we are loved, and that the distinctive biblical response to that love is to love the LORD with all that we are.[8]

> **You are the children [sons] of the LORD your God.** Do not cut yourselves or shave the front of your heads for the dead, for you are a people holy to the LORD your God. Out of all the peoples on the face of the earth, **the LORD has chosen you to be his treasured possession.** (Dt. 14:1–2, my emphasis)

Israel was called to be a distinctive people that resisted the pressure to be like the surrounding nations. The motivation for this distinctiveness is the awareness that the root and source of Israel's identity was their relationship with God. What is clear in the book of Deuteronomy is that God is always the initiator, we are always the respondents. Deuteronomy teaches what is most fully articulated in the New Testament: 'We love because he first loved us.' (1 Jn. 4:19) This is the foundation of the Christian life – an awareness we carry nothing but are ourselves carried by him!

The motivation and capability to love God is based on his prior love for his people. What an encouragement it is to know that God can view us as treasure. God the father looks at his people and where the world sometimes sees trash, he sees treasure. When a person knows that they are precious to someone and valued in their sight nothing else really matters. The fatherless child who looks out at a crowd at the school play, dance show, or sport's day and sees no reassuring face to cheer

---

[8] Dt. 6:5 The Shema, that is at the heart of Old Testament spirituality and forms what Jesus describes as the 'First and greatest commandment', Mt. 22:37, Mk. 12:30, Lk.10:27.

them on feels devalued and worthless. By contrast seeing Dad in the crowd, smiling and cheering you on can make you feel ten feet tall!

An image of identity: Creator (Dt.32:6)

There is nothing quite like Deuteronomy 32. This song is a remarkable celebration of who God is and what he has done.

Firstly, he is our creator. In this picture of Israel's rebellion, the one thing that makes that rebellion offensive to God is that he has formed them. It is a case of biting the hand that feeds them.

> They are corrupt and not his children;
> > to their shame they are a warped and crooked generation.
> Is this the way you repay the LORD,
> > you foolish and unwise people?
> Is he not your Father, your Creator,
> > **who made you and formed you?** (Dt. 32:5-6, my emphasis)

Fatherless people often have identity issues – Who am I and where do I come from? They have missed out on the sense of having been formed; they are disconnected and disorientated. Israel knew who they were and where they came from; the problem was they chose to forget. Such an attitude would be puzzling to the fatherless, who if they had such a connection to their father would cling on to it for dear life.

Secondly, the picture of fatherhood is further developed in the image of an eagle ensuring the security of its chicks in the nest. The act of creation is evoked in the image of the eagle hovering over its young, like the Spirit of God.[9]

> In a desert land he found him,
> > in a barren and howling waste.
> He shielded him and cared for him;
> > he guarded him as the apple of his eye,

---

9 Gen. 1:2.

> **like an eagle that stirs up its nest**
> **and hovers over its young,**
> that spreads its wings to catch them
> and carries them aloft.
> The LORD alone led him;
> no foreign god was with him. (Dt. 32:10–12, my emphasis)

The stirring of the nest is part of the process of encouraging the young to fly. This image of a hovering bird protecting its young is tender and reassuring.

Thirdly the image of the father is developed in one of the major themes of this song: the LORD as the Rock. This image of God as the Rock is seen first in verse 4, and repeated in verses 13, 15, 18, 30, 31, 37. As one wag put it, this is the 'first rock song!' This reassuring imagery reminds us that 'God has the reliability of a crag or cliff onto which you can climb and find certain safety.'

It is in the light of this tender language that we see the tragedy of Israel suffering from such a severe bout of spiritual amnesia that they forgot their distinctive God-given identity. God the Father does not abandon his children; they abandon him, 'You deserted the Rock, who fathered you; you forgot the God who gave you birth.' (v18)

This language is astonishing. The LORD the Rock has fathered them. The image of stability is also an image of source. This ties in with what can be seen in other parts of the Pentateuch, where the image of a rock is used to describe God's provision of life-giving water.[10]

Moses reminds us that no other god in the whole world can offer what the LORD offers his people. 'For their rock is not like our Rock, as even our enemies concede.' (Dt. 32:31) The Father, who is the Rock, is unique. It is his stamp upon us that shapes Israel's unique identity. In 1 Corinthians 10:4 Paul daringly says that the rock Israel drank from was

---

10 Ex. 17:1, 6; Num. 20:1,8,10,11; Dt. 8:15; Is. 32:2, 44:8,21.

Christ.[11] Jesus is the unique revelation of God the Father. In him we find our true significance and security, and the source of true life.

God is Father of the Fatherless

It is not only in Deuteronomy that the LORD is depicted as the defender of the fatherless and their provider. The Psalms have eight references to the fatherless. The fullest is found in Psalm 68:5-6,

> A father to the fatherless, a defender of widows,
>   is God in his holy dwelling.
> God sets the lonely in families,
>   he leads out the prisoners with singing;
>   but the rebellious live in a sun-scorched land.

John Goldingay reminds us that the fatherless had no obvious means of support: 'Through losing the male head of the family, they have lost their security and their place in the community.' Eugene Peterson reminds us how vulnerable the fatherless are and how valuable they are to God:

> The wicked demonstrate their power by oppressing the unfortunate and weak; our righteous God shows his power by dealing with the victim, the outcast, and the defenceless in compassion and love.[12]

I remember being in Riga a week or so after the invasion of Ukraine by Russia. Already Ukrainian refugees were beginning to arrive. In fact, the first person to meet me when I arrived from the airport at the

---

11 I was struck by the statement made in the Messianic Psalm: 'He will call out to me, "You are my Father, my God, the Rock my Saviour." (Ps. 89:26). As Christians we are embraced as full children of the Father. We can address God in the very terms that are used by the Messiah. Lovely!

12 Eugene Peterson, *Praying the Psalms*, (Zondervan: Harper San Francisco, 1993), 12th May.

Latvian Biblical Centre, was a young woman called Helena, surrounded by boxes with her two children nearby. Her situation added poignancy and relevance to my preaching on Psalm 68 that Sunday at Communitas, one of the international churches in Riga. It's striking how much more vivid the Psalter becomes when you have friends in a war zone. I have certainly found that being in Riga at that point brought the reality of war in Ukraine much closer. Reading Psalm 68 that week in preparation for my sermon, connected so many thoughts about the situation that have been rattling away in my mind. Psalm 68 brings a timely word to a generation of Ukrainian children whose dads are putting their lives on the line fighting for their country; some of their fathers are not going to make it home; that is going to leave a lot of fatherless children.

What strikes me is how the view of God in this psalm is so exalted. He is the sovereign Lord who rules over all. He is the Lord of history, to whom we can pray with confidence the words of Psalm 68:30, 'Scatter the nations who delight in war.'

Yet this very God, the warrior who scatters his enemies, is the one who attends lovingly to the vulnerable. As Derek Kidner puts it, 'it [Psalm 68] bears witness to its grasp of this reality, this union of immense power and intense care.'[13] Timothy Keller encourages us to retain this healthy balance: 'If our prayer life discerns God only as lofty, it will be cold and fearful—if it discerns God only as a spirit of love, it will be sentimental.'[14]

That, of course, is the wonder of the Old Testament portrait we have of God. He is the transcendent creator, but he is also the tender father. He is the lofty Lord of Heaven and Earth, but he is also the God who offers us fatherly love and care.

> Fatherlike He tends and spares us;
> Well our feeble frame He knows.

---

[13] Derek Kidner, *Psalms 1-72*, (IVP: Leicester, 1973) p.245
[14] Timothy Keller, *My Rock My Refuge*, (Hodder & Stoughton: London, 2015), p.151.

In His hands He gently bears us,
Rescues us from all our foes.
Praise Him, praise Him,
praise Him, praise Him,
Widely as His mercy goes.[15]

Conclusion

Reflecting on what we have discovered in the Old Testament about God as Father, it is useful to pause for a while to think about the implications for what might be expected of human fathers.

> While OT writers do not overtly present God as a model for human fathers to emulate, the portrait of God as Father obviously includes some of the things that fathers are expected to do for their children.[16]

We live in a world where some look for a rock under their feet but find only quicksand. Reflecting on God the Father in the Old Testament opens a window on how human dads might be attentive and committed to be there for their children. Doing so will enable our children to know who they are, where they come from, and where they are going.

Tragically millions of children have experienced none of these things!

Questions

1) What characteristics of God as Father have particularly struck you as you have read this chapter? How has it made you think differently about what it means to be a father?

---

15 Henry Lyte, 'Praise my Soul the King of Heaven', public domain
16 Diane G. Chen, *God as Father in Luke-Acts*, Studies in Biblical Literature 92 (Peter Lang Inc., International Academic Publishers; 2006), p.86.

2) If you are a parent, how could you reflect more of the character of God the Father in your approach to parenting?

3) If there was one thing you could do to serve the fatherless today, what would it be?

Prayer

Father God, I marvel at how you have revealed yourself to me.

> I will proclaim the name of the LORD.
> > Oh, praise the greatness of our God!
> He is the Rock, his works are perfect,
> > and all his ways are just.
> A faithful God who does no wrong,
> > upright and just is he. (Deut. 32:3-4)

I thank you that you are the rock from which living water flows and you have given me life. I thank you that you are the secure rock on which my feet have a firm foundation. I thank you that when other 'rocks' fail, you remain ever faithful and true.

I thank you Father that you carry me, nurture me, lead me, and train me. I thank you Father that you see me as your treasure: the apple of your eye. I delight in your love and tenderness.

I thank you for the love that will never let me go and will always lead me home. Help me to love you with heart, soul, mind, and strength. Help me to follow you gladly, faithfully, and fully.

I pray for all of us who are fathers to reflect your heart in the way we approach parenthood. May our children feel the preciousness, tenderness, and security of our love in their lives.

In Jesus' name. Amen

Actions

Think of ways how what we have learned about the Fatherhood of God could help you view your relationships differently.

Find out more about how to prayerfully support the fatherless.

'Are you like the string of human fathers I've experienced, or are you something else? Are you like the first father who couldn't be bothered to lay eyes on me?
　Are you like the daddy I loved who left me?
　Are you like the ill-equipped stepfather who left me?
　Maybe you're like that first father who, decades later he didn't even want the second chance he'd been given.' (Margot Starbuck)

'I never knew my father or my mother. I remember once when I was little, the topic came up over dinner with guests; grandfather said Ausma had gone overseas with some circus act and disappeared without trace, like a pebble down a well. After that I'd often peer terrified down the damp and darkened walls of our well, afraid I'll see a drowned woman.' (Zigmunds Skujins)

Chapter 7 ~ Interview: Fatherless in Latvia ~ The influence of culture

Frequently our earthly experiences, which are affected by the culture we live in, serve as the lens by which we perceive our heavenly Father, clouding our understanding of the fatherhood of God. One of my former colleagues at the Latvian Biblical Centre, Ester Petrenko, has written the commentary on Ephesians in the *Central and Eastern European Bible Commentary*. Part of her brief was to read this biblical letter against the background of the country where she was working at the time. She writes:

> After the Second World War, Latvia became a predominantly matriarchal society. Mothers became overprotective of their sons and pushed their daughters to achieve more than they themselves have done, raising a generation of men perceived as weak and indecisive and a generation of strong women.[1]

---

1 Ester Petrenko, 'Ephesians', *Central and Eastern European Bible Commentary*, Corneliu Constantineanu (Author, Editor) & Peter Penner (Author, Editor), (Langham Global Library: Carlisle, 2022), p.1443.

I interviewed a Latvian woman who is fatherless and now works to promote fostering and adoption services. I began by asking about the accuracy of the Ester Petrenko quote.[2]

Interview Five

- Is that an accurate picture of Latvian society?

Can I share an amusing story: my husband and I watch the news, and there is a country couple being interviewed about one thing and another. Usually there is a pale looking shadow of a husband at the back and a vibrant wife in the front. He is monosyllabic, or maybe he doesn't say anything at all. My husband said that this is such a typical scene on the Latvian news.

I think it is also a bit generational; the post-war generation possibly went that way because a lot of the men died in the war or were sent to Siberia and the remnant was left. I don't want to say that they were a remnant but [there were] implications of a large amount of the population being sent away.

There can be things passed down from generation to generation, like learning to keep your head down. I think that every segment of society encourages that, apart from sports. If you speak too much or speak your mind you get a bad press. The result is that men only express their opinions aggressively or do not express them at all.

- How do you see these trends reflected in your work?

I don't have hard data but speaking from observation, there are a lot of foster families, where it is the woman's idea and the man is standing in the background supporting the wife, or maybe not supporting her at all. The woman does the work of a 'saviour' or missionary, and the man stands back.

---

2   Interview conducted on 30th May 2023.

- How does this feed into the situation that creates the need for fostering?

Typically, the father was absent, or struggling with mental health resulting from addictions. Thus, the wife has historically been head of the family. When I was growing up, I didn't have a father and I thought I was normal because nobody had a father, or the father was drunk or in jail.

- What is the first thing that comes into your mind when you hear the word 'father'?

God. I don't really have any other reference point. Having a father who is invisible is quite a stretch for a human being. I had to work from a vacuum into something more substantial. There have been men in my life that have been fatherly figures, but not many. There is a longing for someone to step in and become that for me. But at this point I am reconciled to the fact that it is not going to happen. So, I must make the relationship with God that counts. I understand all the right words and phrases about God being your father and all that, but to grow into that does not happen automatically.

- Some say that what is broken and missing about us because we do not know our fathers doesn't entirely get fixed and replaced. How would you describe the fatherhood deficit that you have felt in your life?

The physical part: being held. A husband can only go so far in compensating for this. It is not appropriate for a wife to expect from a husband what only a father can give. What I missed was that there was someone to take care of me. I had a friend who grew up in a very healthy family, whose problem was that she thought her father was a god. She was so focused on her own father's love and capability that she found it difficult to turn to God. Her son got really ill, and her father could not fix it.

It is hard to ask an invisible being to come and fill this vacuum; sometimes God has done that for me, but there is always going to be a lack and longing. I have lost hope that a human being will largely fulfil that longing. I think that there is a danger to be always looking for that and to start inappropriate relationships.

- Without an obvious blueprint for being a father how have you approached being a wife and a mother?

I think it has made me look at men as a kind of foreign species, but that is something that God has healed, so that I don't feel awkward around men.

- Tell me a bit about your experience of your father. Was he in the words of Jay Blades, 'the man who contributed to my birth'?

Yes exactly. That's my father. He and my mum had a big age difference, she was 16 years old, and he was in his early thirties, and had had a family before. He was an alcoholic. They lived together for a while, I was born, and he continued to be an alcoholic, so my mum got up and left at some point, when I was about two months old. I never remember seeing him since, even though my mum says that when I was four, we ran into him in the street. She exchanged words with him, but I do not have that memory. He died when I was 12, so I did not have a single contact with him but do have some pictures.

My mother's father was also an alcoholic. He lived with us. He was kind and loving. He was dealing with some deep mental health issues, but he would fix things around the house. He and my mum had a tense relationship because they were both stubborn and opinionated.

- How has your background filtered into being an adoptive mother?

I began to realise this past year as my daughter has begun to leave home and travel independently, and while doing that she has been rejected by some people. Her going through the emotions of that has triggered all kinds of emotions in me. I feel as though I have dealt with that already but now feel that in some ways I am back where I started. It has been interesting to go through this with therapists and see how deep a trace this leaves in my life.

- Do you ever think of how your biological father might have contributed to shaping you as a person?

He's Russian. My temperament, drive and assertiveness doesn't come from my mother's side. My looks come from my mother but the way I am made up on the inside is from him. I was thinking that if he had not been an addict, he would have had many qualities that the addiction had covered. So, I am thankful for those qualities that I have, although they were not always helpful to me as a child because I tended to take over because there were so many things that she was afraid to do.

- If you could communicate one thing about what it feels like to be fatherless, what would it be?

In the family picture there is a big gap, and there is a profound feeling of being alone. It is as if there is no supportive figure with you. For me there were also problems with my mum, so it felt at times as if both parents were not there.

- What strategies have helped you develop as a person who is fatherless?

Thankfully God does not abandon you and he is there. I have reached a point in my relationship with God where that feeling of aloneness is not there. One of the ways I have been helped is to see that I am weak. I am not strong enough to handle this; I must admit that this is ok.

- In what ways have your experiences of life and fatherhood helped you in your work, and how has it hindered you?

Maybe I will start with hindered because it is easier to answer. I think it is the 'Messianic feeling'. I can sometimes assume that the people I meet who are alone can be fixed by me stepping in.

When I started therapy in 2004 after my first encounter with depression, (although I had probably had it before but did not know what it was), the therapist kept bring up the subject of fatherlessness, but I kept resisting it. I slowly began to realise that this issue was the huge elephant in the room.

Once I began to open up, there was layer upon layer of pain that surfaced in my life. It became clear that this was the biggest problem in my life, and I ought to deal with it.

- Do you think there is an awareness of this issue in the church, and how important it is?

No. There seems to be more of an emphasis on this theme in the Catholic Church. In the Baptist churches, I don't want to say there is an unhealthy attitude, but there are a lot of young families. Fathers are growing into their roles and learning how to be fathers. Yet for people who did not have that there is the question: 'Is this being glorified right now in the church? What about me, I'm a single mother with a child?'

In church when people give their testimonies and talk about not having a father, it can be glossed over.

- How has your experience made you view your husband in his role as a father?

I think that there is a lot of confusion. I don't have a real blueprint of what it is to have a father in a family. I had conflicting pictures in my mind. There was the man who came home, threw off his shoes and smelly socks, and sat down to watch TV, and there was the glorified picture of a Christian man, who is calling his daughter a little princess. My husband's father was an orphan, so he had a father, but one that was very wounded. For us it was easier with our two biological children, who are boys. We know what to do with them, but our adopted daughter was another story. She has very big emotions, which makes proper heart to heart chats more difficult.

- If churches have people converted who come with deep father related issues, how would you advise pastors to deal with these?

Taking care on boundary issues, when people might look for people in the church to form relationships with. There needs to be sensitive emotional intelligence used to seeing how best to enter another person's life. The three key things that people need to know is that the other person is saying: I see you; I hear you and I cherish you.

- When you read the Bible, what are the stories that encourage you, and what are the ones that disturb you?

All the pictures about God being like a father and mother really move me. Statements like 'even though your parents abandon you I will be there', really move me. The relationship that Mary Magdalene had with Jesus, and the relationship between Mary and Jesus are very moving. The Prodigal Son is very helpful.

I sometimes think of whether it is better to have no father and no blueprint or is it better to have a father who disappoints or hurts us.

✳ ✳ ✳

One young man in Latvia who grew up with a sometimes cruel and often absent father talks about how the experience made him confused about his own identity. He was disorientated by the broken relationship with his father. This young man speaks about the transformative moment in his life when his first child was born. Holding his son for the first time helped him to see that the cycle of fatherlessness could be broken. Becoming a father gave him a loving relationship with a person who was biologically connected to him. Sometimes in life we begin to receive love when we learn to give love.

Questions

1) Different cultures have different experiences of the issue of fatherlessness. It does seem to be a particular feature of Post-Soviet Bloc Countries but, as we have seen, is prevalent in one way or another globally. What local and national cultural influences impact issues of fatherlessness and fatherhood in your community?

2) How might you contribute to breaking the cycle of fatherlessness?

Prayer

Father God, thank you for the words of Psalm 27:10: 'Though my father and mother forsake me, the LORD will receive me.'
I cannot begin to say how much those words mean to those whose father, and sometimes their mother has gone absent without leave. Your welcome, love and support has provided roots and foundations where they have been ripped out and destroyed. To call you 'Father', and to rest in your fatherly care has transformed my life.
I pray for all those who feel ignored and abandoned by their fathers. Provide them with loving support networks and help them as they seek to break the cycle as they build their own family relationships.
I pray for good fathers and good father-figures in the lives of a fatherless generation so that they can see another narrative in life.
In Jesus' name Amen.

Action

If your relationship with your father is similar to those written about in this chapter, reflect on ways that you can break the cycle of fatherlessness in your life. Consider too whether you might need to seek counselling to work through the issues that spring out of the experience of fatherlessness.

Churches have a role in reaching out to a fatherless generation and so need to recognise the cultural influences that contribute to people's experiences. Think about ways that your church could be more attuned to this issue and practical ways that you could assist the fatherless to come to know God as their Father and be equipped to build healthy relationships with others.

Think too of using the letter to the Ephesians, with its strong emphasis on community, as a catalyst for building the church as an agent of transformation in individuals, families and societies.

'Thank you for the Josephs of this world who are content to do the will of God and remain ordinary.' (Lenski)

'How is it that we cannot drive a car on our own without taking a test, but we can become a father with no preparation at all?' (John Woods)

'If I have the smile of God, all other frowns are inconsequential.' (Tim Keller)

Chapter 8:
Human fathers in the biblical story ~ New Testament

Less attention is given to fathers in the New Testament than in the Old Testament. Perhaps that is because the focus of attention in the New Testament is on one particular father and son combination: God the Father and Jesus the Son. Their unique relationship will be explored more fully in a later chapter. However, there are other fathers whose stories feature in the New Testament.

I am always drawn to the courage and bold persistence of Jairus the synagogue leader who earnestly pleads for Jesus to come and attend to his 12-year-old daughter, who is dying. It is moving to trace the roller coaster of emotions he experiences as he risks his reputation in the community by appealing to Jesus in the first place, encounters frustrating delay and then the devastating news of her death, before being elated by Jesus bringing his little girl back to life (Mt. 9:18-26; Mk. 5:21-43; Lk. 8:40-56). This is an example of a girl who was far from being fatherless; her dad is clearly devoted to her. Some say that every little girl is a princess in the eyes of her daddy. If only that were always the case!

We see another example of a father who cares deeply in the story of the second sign performed by Jesus in the Gospel of John, the healing of an official's son (Jn. 4:43-54). There is something beautiful and tender about these two fathers, who are alive to the vulnerabilities of their children and try to move heaven and earth to get Jesus to make a difference in their lives.

Perhaps my favourite father story is the brief reference to the family of Philip the Evangelist.

> Leaving the next day, we reached Caesarea and stayed at the house of Philip the evangelist, one of the Seven. He had four unmarried daughters who prophesied. (Acts 21:8-9)

Four unmarried daughters! How did he ever get into the bathroom? I love the way that these young women each felt the freedom announced on the Day of Pentecost: 'your sons and daughters will prophesy.' (Acts 2:17) There is something beautiful about a dad who encourages his children to flourish by being the people that God has designed them to be. The fatherless tend to have reduced lives, but a child with a good father is given the space to breathe and develop, a helping hand, a shoulder to cry on and a role model to follow.

In this chapter I would like to concentrate on two individuals who help us to think about the place of fathers in society.

Joseph, earthly father to a special son.

What an intriguing character is Joseph the carpenter of Nazareth. I have a soft spot for Joseph, one of the significant players at the beginning of the Christian story, but one who does not have a speaking role. Joseph may not need to learn any lines, but he does learn to play his part. It is difficult to know exactly how to describe his relationship to Jesus. Even the way his role is introduced in Scripture is unusual. In Matthew's account of the genealogy of Jesus we read '…and Jacob the father of Joseph, the husband of Mary, and Mary was the mother of Jesus who is called the Messiah.' (Mt. 1:16)

Jesus is counted as part of Joseph's family line, but it could not be made plainer in the gospels that the only real biological parent of Jesus is Mary, his birth mother. Matthew's Gospel is clear, Joseph is not the biological father of Jesus. Nowhere in the New Testament is Joseph described as the father of Jesus, although he and Mary are referred to as Jesus' 'parents' (Lk. 2:41, 43). In formal and legal terms this is how he was viewed. The crowds ask:

> 'Isn't this the carpenter's son? Isn't his mother's name Mary, and aren't his brothers James, Joseph, Simon and Judas? (Mt. 13:55)

What is clear is that Joseph takes the place of a 'surrogate father' to Jesus. Anyone who has had experience of a blended family will not find it difficult to admire Joseph. It takes courage to take on a baby that is not your own.

Joseph is a man who is committed to doing everything by the book. Joseph is an ordinary man who struggles with the storyline, yet he is a good man. He is engaged to Mary; engagement was something more official in the ancient world than in contemporary Western society. It was a formal nuptial agreement that required a formal legal break (a divorce) to end it. Joseph discovers that his fiancée is pregnant, but he does not want to turn an unpromising situation into a worse one. Joseph could have blown his top as soon as he saw the smoking gun, and Mary could have ended up like the woman in John 8:1-11, surrounded by a group of angry men with stones in their hands. But Joseph was a good man and 'did not want to expose her to public disgrace, he had in mind to divorce her quietly.' (Mt 1:19).

The story is so familiar from our carol services that we might fail to take on board what a remarkable thing is going on in the life of Joseph.

> This is how the birth of Jesus the Messiah came about: his mother Mary was pledged to be married to Joseph, but before they came together, she was found to be pregnant through the Holy Spirit.

> Because Joseph her husband was faithful to the law, and yet did not want to expose her to public disgrace, he had in mind to divorce her quietly. But after he had considered this, an angel of the Lord appeared to him in a dream and said, "Joseph son of David, do not be afraid to take Mary home as your wife, because what is conceived in her is from the Holy Spirit. She will give birth to a son, and you are to give him the name Jesus, because he will save his people from their sins." All this took place to fulfil what the Lord had said through the prophet: "The virgin will conceive and give birth to a son, and they will call him Immanuel" (which means "God with us").
>
> When Joseph woke up, he did what the angel of the Lord had commanded him and took Mary home as his wife. But he did not consummate their marriage until she gave birth to a son. And he gave him the name Jesus. (Mt. 1:18-25)

Joseph does the right(*eous*) thing! Tom Long is surely correct in seeing Joseph as a model for the Christian life.

> He learns that being truly righteous does not mean looking up a rule in a book and then doing the 'right thing'; it means wrestling with the complexities of a problem, listening for the voice of God, and then doing God's thing.[1]

Joseph stepped into the gap and became the significant earthly male figure in the early life of Jesus. Joseph is a good man; well, you wouldn't expect that God would trust his son to any other kind of man, would you?

What made Joseph change his mind about divorcing Mary quietly?

---

[1] Thomas G Long, *Matthew*, (Westminster John Knox: Louisville, 1997), p.14.

Thinking

'But after he had considered this' (Mt. 1:20). Joseph never speaks a word in the gospel, but his action is crucial to God's work of salvation through Jesus. He does not speak but he does reflect on what is going on. It is fascinating to contrast this with the other human father in the nativity story. Zechariah, who like Joseph is described as 'righteous',[2] is also given a message concerning a miraculous birth. Zechariah stumbles with incredulity at the angel's message and as a result remains silent until his son John is born. Two silent men. One a priest trained to expect God to do unexpected things in the world but at the critical moment stumbling at the first fence. The other a carpenter who is used to communicating with his hands, letting his actions speak. This artisan thinks deeply about this complex and mysterious situation and concludes that God must be up to something.

Dreaming

Allen Callahan drew my attention to the similarities between Joseph the adoptive father of Jesus and Joseph in the Old Testament:

> He receives and interprets dreams (Mt.1:20; 2:13,19; compare Gen. 37:5-10; 40 - 41), and he sojourns in Egypt in accordance with a divine plan (Mt. 2:13-15; compare Gen. 39 - 50).[3]

Perhaps the fact that Joseph is open to receiving direction for life in a dream makes him a less one-dimensional figure. Such dreams do not come along every day, but Joseph knows when God is giving him a nudge and taking the hint, he ready to act promptly on them.

---

2 Lk. 1:6 (The whole story is recorded in Lk. 1:5-25; 39-45; 57-66.
3 Allen Callahan, 'Joseph, Story of, History of Interpretation' (p.p. 394-396), *New Interpreter's Dictionary of the Bible Volume 3*, (Abingdon: Nashville, 2008), p.395.

Believing

We know where babies come from, Matthew knew how babies are made, Joseph knew about human reproduction; we must not view biblical characters as primitives who merely accept miracles because they are simple folk. Joseph is open to God; he believes what the Angel of the Lord says to him in a dream: 'Joseph son of David, do not be afraid to take Mary home as your wife, because what is conceived in her is from the Holy Spirit.' (Mt. 1:20b)

Joseph is fearless in the face of the unknown, he does the right thing, he stands by Mary, copes with danger, arranges the escape to Egypt and looks after Jesus. The gifts of gold, frankincense and myrrh brought by the Magi must have come in handy, but we assume that Joseph used his skill as a carpenter (perhaps something more like a jobbing builder), skills much in demand in Egypt, to provide for his family.

Luke 2:40-52 opens a unique window on the childhood of Jesus. It details the interaction between Joseph and Mary and the 12-year-old Jesus. Luke, relating his Jesus-missing-on-holiday story, concludes his brief account with a bird's-eye view of family life in Nazareth:

> Then he went down to Nazareth with them and was obedient to them. But his mother treasured all these things in her heart. And Jesus grew in wisdom and stature, and in favour with God and man. (Lk. 2:51–52)

Whilst Joseph was not Jesus' biological father, he does fulfil a vital parental role in his life. If Jesus developed in wisdom, physically, spiritually, and socially, who shaped him? Dads teach their children stuff; their contribution to the development of boys is particularly vital. Where else will a boy learn to be a man?

Timothy

The other character who stands out for me in the New Testament is Timothy. He is a complex man, who appears to be fragile, self-conscious, and vulnerable. Timothy also seems to have an inferiority complex, what sounds like a nervous tummy, and feelings of anxiety.[4] Could this have been a result of his relationship with his father? We are introduced to Timothy's home situation in the Book of Acts.

> Paul came to Derbe and then to Lystra, where a disciple named Timothy lived, whose mother was Jewish and a believer, but whose father was a Greek. The brothers at Lystra and Iconium spoke well of him. Paul wanted to take him along on the journey, so he circumcised him because of the Jews who lived in the area, for they all knew that his father was a Greek. (Acts 16:1–3)

Luke describes a divided home. Timothy's home was divided by race and most likely, by religion – his father was a Greek and his mother was a Jew. We are not told the details but reading between the lines this created some practical problems, which included Timothy not being circumcised. This badge of belonging to the Jewish community had not been extended to him. This may have been a case of 'not getting around to it', or might indicate a deeper ideological conflict. We can imagine that this created something of an identity crisis for Timothy; he was probably viewed as too Greek to be a Jew and too Jewish to be a Greek. To be 'uncircumcised' was the insult that Jews used to refer to Gentile men, who were perceived to be unclean, impure, and unblessed.

At the beginning of Paul's second letter to Timothy Paul refers to the faith of Timothy's mother and grandmother but says nothing about his father. There is no further mention of Timothy's father after Acts 16, so it is probably fair to assume he had died while Timothy was young.

---

4 1 Tim. 4:12; 5:23; 2 Tim. 1:7

I pay attention to people when they talk about their childhood. When they only talk about their mother and siblings, more often than not this is a tell-tale sign that their father has gone missing in one way or another. Perhaps Timothy was in a similar position. Blair Linne explains that, 'The trauma of fatherlessness wiggles its way into other areas of life. It shows up in anxiety, depression, an inability to express emotions, and struggles with sin.'[5]

Richard Osman is a best-selling novelist and much-loved quizmaster on many television shows, including *Pointless*. Osman spoke candidly on *Desert Island Discs* of his dad leaving the family home when he was 9 years old. He explained that he was called into the lounge, given a glass of squash and told by his father: 'I have fallen in love with someone else, I am leaving; is that ok?' He relates his own struggle with eating disorders that have been one of his coping mechanisms in his life. Osman says that 'there has not been a day in my life since I was 9 that I have not thought about problems with food and how it affects me.'[6] It is important to recognise that addictions of various kinds can be used as coping mechanisms used by those who have been starved of affection and security.

Perhaps some of the issues that Timothy was dealing with in his life were symptoms of the fatherhood deficit in his life. When Timothy became a Christian two significant things happened in his life.

Firstly, he encountered the fatherly love of God for the first time. The writer Lance Pierson writing about Timothy relates a personal story:

> My parents divorced when I was a baby, and I never met my father till I was 33. Many times, during the years in between I ached to know him. I missed the guidance and help my friends found in their fathers. I felt as if I'd had an arm or leg amputated. So, the

---

5 Linne, Blair, *Finding My Father: How the Gospel Heals the Pain of Fatherlessness*, (The Good Book Company: London, 2021), p.88.
6 *Desert Island Discs*, 26/12/2021.

discovery that God was my perfect, ever-present father has often been my favourite part of the Christian good news.[7]

Secondly, Timothy gained a spiritual father figure in the person of the Apostle Paul. Paul took Timothy under his wing and became like a father to him, even referring to him as 'my dear son',[8] and referring to their working relationship as like a father working alongside his son as an apprentice: 'But you know that Timothy has proved himself, because as a son with his father he has served with me in the work of the gospel.' (Phil. 2:22)

It is almost as if Paul is erecting a sign outside his workshop reading 'Missionaries: Paul and Son.' There is something reassuringly liberating about being allowed into another person's life and to feel that someone is interested in you for your own sake. Paul was looking out for Timothy, he invested in his life, and gave him so much more than any other father figure could have given.

Timothy discovered, as so many young men find in our fragmenting society, that good male models are invaluable but hard to find. The actor Mark Strong was born in London, the only child of an Austrian mother and an Italian father. His father left the family when Mark was a baby and has played no part in his life. 'I have no blueprint for being a father,' he says and goes on to speak of his own approach to being a parent to his children: 'You have to give them love and carry them through to adulthood.'[9]

Men need practical help with the basics of what it means to be a man, husband, and father, and how to use time, how to make wise decisions, and how to relate well to others. I will be forever grateful for the Christian men who have shared their time, experience, and wisdom with me.

---

7 Lance Pierson, *In the Steps of Timothy*, (IVP: Leicester, 1995), p.21.
8 2 Tim. 1:2; 2:1.
9 Mark Strong, *Desert Island Discs*, 7th March 2021.

For me, growing up without a father left a lot of gaps in my experience, knowledge, and relationships. In computer terms, the hardware was in place but there were glitches in my operating system, and perhaps some of the wires were missing. God used older men, some who were like fathers, and some who were like wise older brothers, to help me navigate life as a man, husband, and father. Like many fatherless men, I did not have a reliable role model for any of these stages of my life.

One notable role-model was my first church leader, Stanley Griffin. He was a self-taught theologian, who taught me to love Jesus, treasure the word of God, and authentically live out its teachings. He also modelled what it meant to be a man of God, a good husband, and a caring father. Stanley often invited me to join his family for, 'fun, food and fellowship.' Over time I attended the weddings of his three children, was best man at one wedding, and officiated at one. I became Stanley's pastor and finally conducted his thanksgiving service. The memory of those times still moves me to joyful gratitude. This is something that James KA Smith movingly describes:

> There are wounds and scars from the fathers that left but have healed because of the fathers I've found in the body of Christ – who chose me without obligation, loved me without reservation, were present when others were absent – who knew me and yet still loved me.[10]

Every time I read 2 Timothy, I remember the life and sermons of my first 'pastor'. Timothy receives the following directions from his role model, Paul:

> You, however, know all about my teaching, my way of life, my purpose, faith, patience, love, endurance, persecutions, sufferings – what kinds of things happened to me in Antioch, Iconium and

---

10 JKA Smith, *On the Road with Augustine*, p.202.

Lystra, the persecutions I endured. Yet the Lord rescued me from all of them. In fact, everyone who wants to live a godly life in Christ Jesus will be persecuted, while evildoers and impostors will go from bad to worse, deceiving and being deceived. But as for you, continue in what you have learned and have become convinced of, because you know those from whom you learned it, and how from infancy you have known the Holy Scriptures, which are able to make you wise for salvation through faith in Christ Jesus. All Scripture is God-breathed and is useful for teaching, rebuking, correcting, and training in righteousness, so that the servant of God may be thoroughly equipped for every good work. (2 Tim. 3:10–17)

If being fatherless often means feeling that there is something vital that is missing in our lives, having role models that point us to Jesus, teach us how to read Scripture and show us how it is lived out is an invaluable gift. This is the way that God so often comes to those who have a father deficit so that they might be 'thoroughly equipped for every good work.' This means being complete rather than struggling with missing pieces, whole rather than broken, healed rather than wounded. It means being equipped to develop a healthy spiritual life, clear thinking, and consistent practice. In 2 Timothy, the young apprentice is given a word for when he feels daunted by his vulnerability: 'For the Spirit God gave us does not make us timid, but gives us power, love and self-discipline.' (2 Tim. 1:7)

We cannot underestimate the damage done by parental neglect, nor can we value too highly the importance of those who come into our lives and breathe into us the air of hope. Sarah Mullally writes about an example of this:

> In an interview a few years ago, the novelist Rose Tremain spoke movingly about the absence of love that she had felt growing up.

Her father walked out on the family, and she and her sister were packed off to boarding school. As she became an adult, she tried to reach out to her father, who had broken off all contact, to no avail. The rejection was so extreme that, even when she sent him books that she had written, he would return them unread. The only person that she could depend on for affection was her nanny. She said, 'In some miraculous way, maybe because I was shown love by Nan, I was all right. I had a template for how one might love.'[11]

Timothy is being given a template of how to be loved and how to love. Subtly his mentor is gently rewiring his emotional circuitry, so that Timothy can learn to feel secure in a love that will never let him go.

Timothy also is helped to see the source of his strength for the demands of ministry: 'You then, my son, be strong in the grace that is in Christ Jesus.' (2 Tim. 2:1) This is not a call for Tim to be strong in himself; to set his jaw, to grit his teeth, rather it is a call to be inwardly strengthened by grace. The words 'be strong' on their own would be woefully inadequate. Lance Pierson made the comment that: 'He might as well have told a snail to be quick or a horse to fly, as to command a man like Tim to be strong.' It does not help a person who is turned in on themselves to be told to look within themselves, dig deeper and find your inner strength. Here the focus is on the strength of 'grace'; the word that more than any other in the New Testament sums up the initiative and action of God for and in human beings to rescue and remake them, and then equip them for life.

Timothy is also given advice on the importance of training others (2 Tim. 2:2), what to preach and how to preach (2 Tim. 1: 9–14; 2:8–15; 4:1–5), how to avoid distractions (2 Tim. 2:16–18, 22–23; 3:1–9), and how to deal with difficult people (2 Tim. 2:24–26). Such life lessons are precious and invaluable. Sometimes fatherless people are like those preparing to take

---

11 The Times, 6 October 2018 quoted in Sarah Mullally (ed), *Rooted in Love: Lent Reflections on life in Christ*, (SPCK: London, 2020), p.44–45.

an exam, who when they look at their course notes realise that there are huge gaps in their knowledge because these were things that they were not taught. Praise God for those like Stanley who come alongside people like me and helped to plug some of those gaps and pointed to wholeness.

Goodness does not just happen, but when we encounter it in its purest form it melts us. We could all do with the hard parts of our memories being melted. There are many fatherless people out there who could do with seeing a different model of fatherhood. Who will step up to the plate?

Note on father figures in the church

It is important to hear what Jesus says in the Gospels: 'And do not call anyone on earth "father", for you have one Father, and he is in heaven.'(Mt. 23:9) We need to understand the difference between God being father and any human being fulfilling that role. I am never comfortable calling Christian ministers Father this and Father that. Yet Paul is happy to describe his ministry as father-like:

> Even if you had ten thousand guardians in Christ, you do not have many fathers, for in Christ Jesus I became your father through the gospel. (1 Cor. 4:15)

> For you know that we dealt with each of you as a father deals with his own children, encouraging, comforting and urging you to live lives worthy of God, who calls you into his kingdom and glory. (1 The. 2:11-12)

Questions

1) Who are the father figures in your life?

2) Are there distinctive ways that fatherless men and women might need to be supported? Who has mentored you and who are you mentoring?

3) Have you found ways to thank them for what they have meant to you?

4) Paul speaks of the role of a father to be one of 'encouraging, comforting and urging'. How might these terms inform father figures as they interact with their sons and daughters?

Prayer

Father God, thank you for the Josephs of this world, who without making a fuss got on with the job of stepping into the gap to serve your Son as he was born into the world.
Help me to step into the gaps created by a fatherless generation.
Enable me to serve the fatherless so that they can develop and flourish. Provide blueprints of fatherhood to those who have none so that the next generation might have fewer who are wounded.
In Jesus' name. Amen.

Action

Joseph stepped into the role of being a 'dad' to Jesus, Paul fulfilled a vital fatherly role in the life of Timothy. Think of ways that you might do something similar in someone's life. A word of warning in a generation nervous of the abuse of power – it might be best to wait to be invited.

'Yes, he was eighty-eight, but a cataclysmic hole now suddenly gapes open in your life, a part of you snatched away forever ... am writing about my father in the past tense, and I cannot believe I am writing about my father in the past tense.' (Chimamanda Ngozi Adichie)

'No one ever told me that grief felt so like fear. I am not afraid, but the sensation is like being afraid. The same fluttering in the stomach, the same restlessness ... I dread the moments when the house is empty.' (CS Lewis)

'How could the Creator of the world be angry at something in his world? Only if death is an intruder. Death was not in God's original design for the world and human life ... Death is not the way it ought to be. It is abnormal, it is not a friend, it isn't right. This isn't truly part of the circle of life. Death is the end of it. So grieve. Cry.' (Timothy Keller)

'Brothers and sisters, we do not want you to ... grieve like the rest of mankind, who have no hope. For we believe that Jesus died and rose again, and so we believe that God will bring with Jesus those who have fallen asleep in him.' (1 Thessalonians 4:13–14)

Chapter 9 ~ Interviews: Lost too Early

We all know about the inevitability of death. Yet this does not prevent the impact of the death of a loved one from hitting us like a runaway truck. Psalm 90 reminds us of the eternity of God and the mortality of human beings.

> A thousand years in your sight are like a day that has just gone by, or like a watch in the night.
> Yet you sweep people away in the sleep of death – they are like the new grass of the morning:
> In the morning it springs up new, but by evening it is dry and withered. (Ps. 90:4–6)

The longest recorded life span in the Bible, Methuselah at 969 years old, is just shy of 1000 years that are like a day to God. It is like God looking through an upside-down telescope that narrows down to the brevity of human life. From God's perspective the longest human life is a blink of the eye! In theory we all accept that there are limitations to human life, as the Psalmist adds in Psalm 90:

> Our days may come to seventy years, or eighty, if our strength endures;

yet the best of them are but trouble and sorrow, for they quickly pass, and we fly away. (v10)

The phrase 'three score years and ten', from the Authorized Version of verse 10, has entered our language. It underlines the fact that the Lord is infinite and that we by contrast are limited to space and time; we are mortal. I am reminded of the words that I have spoken hundreds of times in funeral services: 'In the midst of life we are in death.'

Yet what happens when the people we love die well before that allotted span of seventy or eighty? We can feel cheated when loved ones are lost too early. One of the things that I have needed to do as a Christian minister conducting funerals is to come to terms with my own death. I need to be honest about the fact that I will die and that other people around me will die. I have taken funerals for people who have died at over one hundred years old. I have been at the graveside when two tiny shoebox-sized coffins were placed in the ground after the death of twin boys, who lived for less than a week. I have wept with families of those who have buried wives and husbands, sons and daughters, mothers and fathers who have gone before their time. JKA Smith writes in his book *How to Inhabit Time*:

> To be temporally aware of our creaturehood is to wear mortality comfortably. To live mortally, we might say, is to receive gifts by letting go, finding joy in the fleeting present.[1]

There is a wrong kind of 'living in the moment', that disregards the need to have any sense of an eternal perspective on life. Yet the idea of living in the gift of the moment that God gives us is a helpful one. When we think of our lives and the lives of those we love as gifts we begin to recognise that as with all of God's gifts, they are not something we deserve or can presume upon but are entirely dependent upon the

---

1 JKA Smith, *How to Inhabit Time*, (Brazos: Grand Rapids, 2022), p.100.

giver. Job, faced with the catastrophic whirlwind of loss that snatched away his children, property and health, shows heart-cracking grief. Tearing his robe and shaving his head, Job stands before God as naked as the day he was born and speaks out but also comes to this astonishing testimony:

> "Naked I came from my mother's womb, and naked I shall depart. The LORD gave and the LORD has taken away; may the name of the LORD be praised." (Job 1:21)

This response seems too good to be true, and we see from Job 3 that the searing pain, frustration and probing questions are not far beneath the surface.

Former President Joe Biden's five-decade career in politics began in 1972 with him being elected aged 29 as the senator for Delaware. He had married his university sweetheart, they had two toddler sons and a baby daughter. Weeks before heading to Washington his wife and daughter were killed in a car accident. One of his sons, Beau, died in 2016 from a rare form of brain cancer. Catholic Biden said: 'I felt God had played a horrible trick on me, and I was angry.'

Biden keeps a simple 'Hagar the Horrible' cartoon from *The Sun* newspaper, that was sent to him by Piers Morgan. It was one of the things that helped him overcome these two devastating family tragedies: One panel of the cartoon depicts a Viking stranded on an island with his ship sinking in the distance; he looks up to the heavens and asks: 'Why me?' in the second panel a voice from the heavens asks: 'Why not?'[2]

We live in an age of entitlement; if trouble strikes, we ask: 'What did I do to deserve this?' When things are going well nobody asks: 'What did I do to deserve the good things that have fallen into my life today?' If we lose everything, we still have the one who has given us everything.

---

2 www.dailymail.co.uk/debate/article-8924671/PIERS-MORGAN-cartoon-Joe-Biden-told-helped-survive-two-family-tragedies.html accessed 13/12/2024

This is counter-intuitive for most people in the twenty-first century. Yet as the quotation from JKA Smith reminded us, an alternative attitude would be to hold on to God's temporal gifts lightly, enjoying the gift of the moments we have with people and always being ready to let go.

Fatherlessness comes in a variety of forms; death is one of them. There are some people whose fathers died before their time, others are orphans because one or both parents have died or are missing. This can often happen in the chaotic aftermath of war or famine.

In this chapter I have conversations with a variety of people who are fatherless because they have lost their dads 'too early'. These range from John Kirkby, the founder of Christians Against Poverty (CAP), who lost his father when he was 18; one Christian leader who lost his dad as a boy; a woman, whose dad died just before she got married; and two men whose dads died around the time when they became dads for the first time themselves. It is instructive to see what these five have in common but also how they have processed their losses differently. It is always important to see that people respond to loss in various ways and that there is no one-size fits all way to deal with it. The first of these interviews, by kind permission is not anonymous.

Interview Six[3]

I had bumped into John Kirkby and his wife Lizzie on a visit to the Island of Jersey. John founded Christians Against Poverty (CAP). I was interested in discovering what impact his experience of fatherlessness had on his work with CAP. As has happened a few times with this book, the interview went in a direction I had not anticipated.

- What is the first thing you think of when you hear the word 'father'?
It is bittersweet. On the good side, he was an incredibly kind, generous, gentle man.

---

3 Interview conducted on 6th September 2023.

He was mad-professor-like and was constantly inventing things. He passed away when I was 18, but for the last five years I was not the son he deserved. Then there was the sense that I did not have him in my life anymore. It is 43 years ago since he passed and even now once a month or so I just go: 'Oh Man!' He did not meet my wife my kids, or my grandkids. He never saw me turn my life around. He deposited some good things in my life; self-assurance, self-esteem.

- You say that at 18 you were pretty much on your own.

My dad always got better, until he didn't. Within three or four months of my dad's death my mother ended up in a mental institution. Seven months later my mum came home but I was on my way to getting married. I was debt collecting at the time.

- You must have seen a big slice of life there.

I had been an angry violent young man. It was the prevailing culture. I could look after myself, I was a fast runner, and I could see trouble before it arrived. At 15 I left school and got a job in a paint factory, telling them I was 16. I built a business in stealing paint; I would flog it in pubs. I was a sandwich boy at the factory delivering 80 sandwiches in the morning and at lunchtime. I went into the local sandwich shop saying I had orders for 80 sandwiches, what price are you going to do them for? I made more money on the sandwich run than in my factory pay.

- Something of that entrepreneurial spirt has now been used for God.

Yes, it is amazing how God has turned that around. I also learned how to read people and situations. This has also been put to good use. I am a front-line police chaplain; in that environment I can see when things are going to kick off.

- In that work and your work with CAP you must have encountered people who were fatherless in several ways. How did your experience help you to come alongside them?

I brought to these situations my own journey toward disaster in life. My first marriage failed, I was in huge debt, abandoned by everyone, and then finding faith amid all that. This has produced in me a compassion for people. Four years after becoming a Christian I founded CAP.

- How have you had input into families that are broken, who have dads who are absent or disengaged?

My major work has been building the charity up, but I continued to work with clients for several years. I met a lady 20 years ago, who was cutting my hair. I got to know her and find out about her fatherless background. She found Christ and I call her our 'sixth daughter.' She is now married with a little baby.

Family has been massively important to me. I have five kids and three grandkids and have a great relationship with all of them. My wife has been amazing in embracing my two girls from my previous marriage. My dad was 40 when I was born and I was 40 when my son Tom was born, so I have walked the path my father would have walked. I think about what it must have been like to deal with me. My son is amazing. When I got my CBE, I asked if all five kids could go. Our children can do a lot of relational rewiring in our lives.

- Do you think that the church gets the challenge of fatherlessness?

This is the first conversation I have had about fatherlessness in 30 odd years. I am sure that if I needed help people would have been there. I am very conscious around Mother's Day and Father's Day. In our church in Bradford more than 50% of the people will not have a dad or a mum, or their recollection of their dad or their mum will either be traumatically sad, or they cannot comprehend the words Father God with their experience of being fathered. I was a single parent for 2½ years so am sensitive to these issues. What could be worse than having a father who is horrendous to you? Fatherhood was in and around all the issues that led to my insomnia, which I had help with.

- If you were starting up the pastoral life again, what might this conversation inform in terms of your approach to your preaching and pastoral care?

I think that is done anyway. You either go looking for people who need help or respond to those who know they need help and come forward. I guess that most of it would be for those who come forward.

In some communities where CAP works there are three generations who have no meaningful father figures. How do we preach on fatherhood? Church is middle-class. There will be different parenting issues. Yet if you are a billionaire or have nothing, being fatherless will play a part in who you are.

My memories of my father are so positive. Fishing, damming rivers ... I am an awful blueprint of a son. My mum died of cancer in 2005 aged 85. She had 30 years as a widow. I couldn't bring myself to ask my mum about what my dad thought of me. As she was dying, I wheeled her to a little park near where she lived, and I said: 'Mum I have got to ask you a question. This is a question I have been waiting 30 years to ask you: What did my dad think of me?' She said: 'The more you were in trouble, the more he loved you and he always knew you would do well.' Wow!

I have been involved as a police chaplain in talking to many people who are bereaved. When I get an opportunity, I will say: 'I am not sure how it is for you, but this is how it has been for me.' When my dad died probably within a few years I had a chasm, a massive hole in my life, that I tried to fill with everything. Now I would say that there is still an indentation in my life. The hole is filled, the soil is over it, it is grassed but although no one else will notice it, but for me there is an indentation.

Jesus is in glory with marks in his hands. Knowing God does bring healing, but it does not replace what we don't have humanly.

One church leader hosted a BBQ at his house – he knew I couldn't afford to bring anything. So, he left a bag of stuff in the kitchen and told me to come in to pick it up so I could bring something. I had a bit of dignity as a dad. That is going to win people for Christ. There are many different versions of fatherlessness. Eroding fatherhood in our society devalues the currency of fatherhood and makes it more difficult for people to get their heads around the fatherhood of God.

Interview Seven: Losing a father as a child

- **How old was your Dad when you were born?**

In his 50s. He had been married before and had four children – then his wife died. I was nine when he died, so he would have been in his early 60s.

It is all dark history – that is part of the issue when you lose your father when you are young. I couldn't tell you the colour of his eyes or how tall he was, or the tone of his voice. All I have is faded pictures!

I guess he was of a generation where men did not have lots of interaction with their children. I think he used to play games with me. The photos I have shown him holding me. He had quite a responsible job and was active in church life, so he was a busy man. In the 1960s men tended to be out at work and your mum tended to be with the children. I have no memory of him actually doing anything with me. I have no recollections; which surprises me.

- **Was his death sudden?**

Yes. He was managing director of a group of engineering companies and those days asbestos was used frequently in industrial units. His first wife died at 54 of throat cancer, which was quite likely caused by shaking his clothing out in the garden. He then died of lung cancer, having never smoked in his life.

- **Then your mum remarried?**

When I was about fourteen or fifteen years old, she married my stepfather. It is a big thing to have a teenager come into your life in these circumstances but over time we became very close.

- **When you hear the word 'father' what is the first thing that comes into your mind?**

I became a Christian when I was in my mid to late teens. I started to go out with the girl who is now my wife. She kept me on the Christian path. I had an unexpected, unrequested and uninvited experience of God. I grew up in the Brethren, which did not encourage talking about experiences of the Holy Spirit. I was at home and had the sense that I should kneel down; so, I did. I can only describe it as being struck by an electric current, with a sense of a very strong white light. I felt enveloped by a white light and a sense of electricity in the room. It lasted for two or three minutes. I had no idea what it was. But it felt as if I was experiencing an unusual sense of the presence of God.

There was a moment during that time when someone prayed for me and I would describe it as being like all the absence of fatherhood was filled with God's presence. I can remember it clearly. I was actually ill in bed after being prayed for, it was such an upheaval. But from that moment on I have never felt the absence of a father in my life. I am 62 now and then I was about 19 years old, and it is no reflection on my earthly father but the proximity I feel to my Heavenly Father is extraordinary.

I didn't have any counselling about these things, I have not really talked to many people about it; you didn't in those days, you just got on with life. Yet I could see the difference in me before and after I prayed. The primary thing of the Spirit is his powerful witness that allows us to cry Abba Father. To feel the fatherhood of God and no longer feel like orphans.

- **How did you navigate becoming a father yourself?**

You have to ask my son. All I know was I intuitively wanted to be with him. It wasn't a hardship for me. My wife was very good in making sure that I was disciplined about that. Being in the line of work I am in, in church leadership makes it a challenge. When I got home, we would play and invest in him. I felt that whatever I had got I wanted to give to him.

- **Do you think the church is well attuned to people with father issues?**

I think that there has been a lot of ministry emphasis on fatherhood issues. We need to recognise that our experiences of God can be different: for some it is like a Damascus Road experience, for others it is more like an Emmaus Road experience.

Some are sudden like the experience I described but others are more gradual. I think that the local church in its own un-shining glory, its ordinariness, is actually more holistically beneficial for people as the family of God. Some men, who I would regard as my spiritual fathers have had input into my life over many years, often in quite undramatic ways. Their wisdom, advice, and accessibility made the kind of contribution that is often unrecognised.

- **In terms of our own antennae in pastoring and preaching, how does your experience feed into your preaching and pastoral life?**

I am not sure if it is my experience or whether it is the way that God has wired me, but I would say that I tend to intuitively understand people. Losing your father makes you always looking for affirmation, companionship and love. Searching for what you have not had, even if you are not sure what it is.

Interview Eight: Losing a father at life's key turning points

The next brief interview is with a woman who also lost her father as she was about to launch out in life.[4] In the year of this interview, I met another woman who had a mirror image experience of this interviewee. They both lost their dads immediately before their wedding days. To have a father ripped out of the script of their lives at such a point was traumatic and life changing.

- What comes into your mind when you hear the word 'father'?

A feeling of being at ease and safe. Quiet chats. Opportunities to share joys, sorrows, hang-ups, and fears.

- Can you describe your relationship with your dad in ten key words?

Comfortable; mutual respect; openness; trust; relaxed; secure; calm; dependable; unconditional love; able to be taken for granted.

- Tell me about the circumstances that led to your dad's death.

He was never in robust health. Practically all relatives on both sides had died of heart failure. He also had hardening of the arteries which is likely to have been caused by his being a moderate smoker at one time. His illness was largely invisible because he managed it by being realistic about what he could accomplish with the strength/energy he had: he was only ever off work for the usual things like flu. He was a gentle, mild-mannered man which made him susceptible to bullying by stronger personalities. Such a man was his boss. One day they argued, and we believe Dad must have had a heart attack and died on the spot. He was declared dead on arrival at hospital.

---

4 Interview conducted by email.

- How did you process that loss and what has been the long-term impact on the way you now view life?

At the time, I processed his death very badly. Our family has a long tradition of going into denial about unpleasant things and this was my first port of call. In addition, as a young Christian, I had a very superficial understanding of the gospel (and life) and I approached bereavement from the point of view that, as dad was a believer, there could be no reason to grieve! Naturally, I did have to grieve properly, but this didn't happen for a few years after the event. Three big 'life events' during one year (Dad's death, marriage, and a move to a different area of the country) were hard to process and I coped mainly by being depressed for a few years.

Though still inclined to deny unpleasant things, one thing I did acquire was a deeper understanding of the sovereignty of God and the fact that he graciously supplies what I need to handle whatever he gives me to cope with. This is a precious truth. Perhaps inevitably, I have also taken away from this the fact that life is very uncertain, and that sadness is an integral part of the life we live on earth. It has made me think a lot about heaven and I long to be there.

- In what way has the gospel which introduced you to your heavenly Father helped you to find something of what you have lost on earth?

My understanding of God's fatherhood has been one of the greatest areas of growth I have experienced in my Christian life. It has transformed from a view of God who was distant to one who is deeply and intimately committed to my welfare, 'He who did not spare His only Son … How will he not also along with him freely give us all things'? My experience of being fathered is very positive, but I can easily see that my heavenly Father is perfect and also so much more concerned with the details of my life than my lovely earthly one. In addition, he offers me things that my Dad could not give me. My Dad was peace-loving, the corollary of which is a propensity to cowardice: from my heavenly Father I receive protection and security which I could not have from Dad.

Interview Nine: Losing a father unexpectedly and suddenly, as a younger man on the threshold of fatherhood[5]

- **What comes into your mind when you hear the word 'father'?**

Playing football with dad on the field opposite our house growing up. My dad was often busy at work but every so often he and I would go and have a kick about on the field.

- **Can you describe your relationship with your dad?**

My dad was often away at work when I was young, or he got home late in the evening and was tired from driving for hours. He was also often away at weekends playing bridge for his county.

I often think of the time we would spend in the car when my dad would take us on different trips and holidays. He would put music on in the car. I wouldn't say we had a very deep relationship. I remember having a couple of heart-to-hearts with him. One time our best man had forgotten to invite him to my stag do. So, my dad and I went out together on another day. He gave me a bit of advice about marriage and things like that. That was not very common growing up. We got on but we were not particularly close.

- **Tell me about the circumstances that led to your dad's death.**

My mum and dad loved going on holiday. He retired at 53 and saved up enough for him to spend as much time as he could on holiday. They were on holiday for a weekend break. The first thing I heard about his death was a phone call at four o'clock in the morning. It was my sister who was on holiday with them saying that dad had died of a heart attack. Dad was fifty-seven so it was a massive shock. My wife was pregnant with our first

---

5   Interview conducted on 20th November 2023.

child; he knew we had a baby on the way but died in the September and our eldest was born in December.

- What was the impact on you at the time?

I was 29 at the time and found it difficult to process theologically. When my grandfather had died six months before I had had a stark conversation with my dad. My grandad died of pancreatic cancer, and he knew he was going to die. My wife and I had spoken to my mum and dad and said: 'We are going to speak to him about Jesus one last time.' My grandfather had refused to talk about religious things even though he knew that he was dying. I think that this shocked my dad. He had viewed his dad as a reasonable person who had nothing to lose by listening. My dad always said that if he [his father] was going to become a Christian it would be on his deathbed when he would have the most to gain and the least to lose.

It shocked my dad that my grandad wouldn't do that. I told him [dad] that I would not chase him on his deathbed, so my dad said: 'Ok', then I got a phone call from my mum who also said 'ok.' We scheduled an evangelistic session with them two months later; my dad said that he did not believe in miracles or the supernatural and my mother said that she did but did not understand the implications of it. They both went away and read a Gospel. My dad read Luke's Gospel and my mum read John's Gospel. My dad had some questions on the resurrection, so I lent him the book Who Moved the Stone? *by the journalist Frank Morrison. Both my mum and dad read that and then I gave him another book to read, and that was when my dad died. He had started to look into things for the first time. In some ways this was harder because he appeared to respond a bit and then it just stopped. Obviously, we do not know what happened at the last moment of his life. He knew what the gospel was, but it was hard that when he was beginning to respond the opportunity was taken away.*

Soon after, we had a child. I had never been a father before and I missed having the support of my own father there. I felt that quite acutely, my wife had her mum and her dad, but I did not have a dad to go and ask: what do

I do here? We decided to give our eldest son my dad's name as his middle name. We had not intended to do that, but it was a way of honouring him.

- **How did you process that loss and what is the long-term impact on the way you view life?**

We can read in the Bible about God being father and us being his sons and daughters; you can get that intellectually before you have children but there is something about having your own children you begin to understand God's heart a lot better.

- **Is there something about the wound of loss that never seems to go away?**

It is less acutely painful now, but it is still there. It is those times when we have been on holiday and I think back to childhood holidays when my grandad would be there. He, my dad and I would go for a walk, and the girls would do something else.

With me and my boys there is no generation up, so it feels as if something is missing. Music gets me. My dad was into music, 60s-70s bands especially. Sometimes a song will come on and it will be one of my dad's favourite songs and I find myself thinking about my dad and missing him. It doesn't quite go away; it moves to the back of your head, but it is still there. Often it is in the happier moments that the sadness comes in. My dad is not there to see it; he didn't get to see his grandchildren.

- **In what ways have people in the church provided father-like role models to you?**

The person who led me to Christ and the pastor of the church where I was working were brilliant in stepping in to support me. I remember that there was a time when I got really upset and the pastor took me for a drink and sat with me for an hour and just listened. I can't remember if he said anything helpful but just being there actually was really helpful. It is not something that I have actively sought out; I feel that I might be betraying my dad if I did that. My father-in-law has been brilliant as well. He has been something of a cheerleader. He has let me look after his daughter!

- If you were speaking to someone who had lost their dad too soon, what advice would you give them.

I would want to say: 'keep going.' In the sense that it is really easy to be consumed by grief. People know that grief takes time to process. Keep going in the midst of that, keep going to Jesus, and keep trusting in the gospel. It is unnatural for death to be so early, but Jesus is enough even in the midst of that.

- How do you think the church does generally on this issue?

I don't think I have heard it addressed as a subject. My Dad's dad walked out on him when he was 17. He was studying to be an accountant; his mum was in hospital and his dad walked out and ran away with another woman. My dad had to abandon his studies and look after his mum. It is interesting how generationally things go down. I think my dad was affected by that. I never remember my dad taking off his wedding ring; I wonder whether it was because he remembered what his dad did. By common grace he seemed to think we need a circuit break here.

Interview Ten: losing a father when a young man, as the result of a long illness

The final interview is with someone who has processed his loss a bit differently. Flashes of frustrated anger have punctuated the years since the death of his father.[6]

- What is the first thing that comes into your mind when you hear the word 'father'?

I just think of my dad. Authority is the word that comes to mind.

---

6   Interview conducted on 11th September 2023.

- Why is that?

I think of fathers as strong figures, who create structure. My dad was more mysterious than he was familiar to me. I think it was because of a perceived distance in authority between the father and the son, which meant that I always related to him as authority rather than as friend. Dad was born in 1957, I was born in 1983.

I am interested in the subject of fatherhood, in part because I wanted to connect with and understand my dad. I am an extrovert; he was an introvert. As I have grown up, I realise that he was quite shy. He didn't share emotional things; we didn't talk about emotional or inner realities. He was an intellectual, a rationalist, who lived in his head rather than in his heart. He was a practical man whose language was sport.

He tried to instil in me a desire to walk and explore, which I think is part of the male role of father, to push the family outside of the home. I rarely would have seen him cry or express vulnerability. He brought discipline, but he was also the peacemaker, so he was not authoritarian. He was harder to bend than my Mum was to get what I wanted. I was more scared of him than my mum because of the deeper voice and the strength he had. I remember one point where he became so cross with me that he pinned me against the wall. I was a loud hyperactive teenager and was probably not picking up cues from him to quieten down, so he got frustrated and took it out on me. I think that there was often a perceived distance between him and me. Probably because he didn't know how to connect to my heart. I didn't sit still enough for a patient, thoughtful man to engage with me. When we did connect it was around activity like sport. The last five years when he got cancer we began to connect more because we had some shared hobbies, like chess over the internet. He also took interest in a little computer game that we would play together.

- How old were you when your Dad died?

27

- **Did you have much time to prepare for that or was it unexpected?**

I was prepared and I appreciated the amount of time because it meant we connected at a deeper level. If he had died soon after he became ill, when I was 22, I would have been left with a lot more angst. Over the five years I matured, and he was developing some things to talk on and connect on. But, either in my naivety or immaturity I don't think I was aware of how close to the end we were.

I am a person who wants to talk about emotional things and ultimate realities, but he was not interested in talking about those things. I couldn't draw him out in a conversation on those things. Either because of his shyness and fear or he just knew his own mind. He was a convinced secular atheist probably; a humanist he would probably call himself. We never had a conversation about faith or religion. Then I finally got the call from my Mum to say that he was going today. It took me by surprise in the end.

- **What were your life circumstances at the time?**

Just had my first son; he was three months old. I lived away from the family home. I felt that I had brought some joy to my dad's life for the last three months of his life by giving him a grandson. I could tell that this meant the world to him. For me that was very satisfying. I could name him and give him my dad's name as a middle name. Dad could know that an aspect of his legacy could live on in his grandson.

I wanted to share the gospel with him and see him saved. That is my abiding memory over that time. I had given my dad some books, Lee Strobel's Case for Christ; he read it, but he was not searching. I realise that in my attempts to crowbar in the gospel I was not giving myself space to appreciate him. One of the things I felt prompted to do was to write him a letter where I was able to honour him as a father, appreciate all that he had given me as a father, and share the gospel within that. He responded positively but said that there was no need to worry about him. He had given it a lot of thought and said he did not worry about dying.

- **How did you respond to the loss of your dad?**

I wrote something ten years after he died, at the start of the pandemic. It was a surprise to me the strength of emotion ten years on. Processing my thoughts in writing has always been a helpful therapeutic tool for me. After he died, I did try to write something each year to reflect upon my loss. I realised that at the start of the pandemic, that when anxiety based on the circumstances around you hits you, it is disorientating. I recognised that what I wanted was my dad to reassure me and make it OK. One of the things that I was struggling with at the start of the pandemic was that he was not there to do that. I remember writing that expression: 'How dare you f..... die?' It was my way of saying: 'Where are you?' I feel like a scared child and my family is looking to me to get some leadership or comfort. The church that I am pastoring is supposedly looking for reassurance from a pastor figure, but what I wanted at that time for my dad to reassure me and make it OK. The strength of that reaction taught me a lot about my relationship with Father God. The fact that my father was not with me was scaring me. Did that mean that the Father was not there and could not help me?

- **What impact has his loss had on your own sense of identity?**

Even at 27, I was married, and I was a father myself, but I felt fatherless. You tend to associate fatherlessness with a teenager or a child. Fathers are the people you go to when you do not know what to do. We joke that we have got Google, but not everyone wants Google, they want Dad. They will take Google, but they only use it to show their dads what they have done. Everyone wants to impress their dad. You never tire of wanting to hear your dad say: 'Wow. Well done.'

Dad was good at art and three years before he died, he drew me a picture. Two or three years after he died, I took the back off the picture and saw that he had written something on the picture to me. That was a profoundly powerful moment. These were fresh words in the present from a man who had been dead for years. There were words of affirmation, expressing his love for me and saying that he was proud of me. Those words were, to quote Gladiator: 'Like the song of my heart for 1000 years.' There isn't anything close to a father telling you that he is proud of you and loves you.

- What have you missed most?

Not having someone to talk to about money or doing a practical job is a loss for me. When it goes well, I always want to show him. It is an inner gnawing ache within my heart, which as a believer I allow Father God to communicate this reality to me, but I still have a longing for affirmation from my father. As a result, my relationship with my father-in-law has become very important to me. I have looked to him to play some of the parts that my dad used to play.

I have seen it in myself and in others, what we might call the magnetic draw toward father figures. This is something I don't observe in women to the same degree. With the loss of my father, I find myself being a lot more vulnerable to other fathers. Of course, Jesus says that they are not all good shepherds; some of them might be wolves. I have been attracted to vocal men giving me guidance for life, that spoke to my heart in ways that my earthly father could not. Preachers I heard but never met became potential role models. One of the reasons Andrew Tate gained such a following is because he presented himself as a strong father figure to a fatherless generation.

- What impact has his loss had on your own approach to being a father?

I keep swallowing emotion because I don't want to cry. I don't like the loss of control that crying brings. I know what I want to say. I am very aware that I do not know how much time I have. I think that that makes me a lot more deliberate about trying to be as intentional as I can. It probably also means that I am harder on myself when I screw up or when I lose control and fly off in a rage. I think that I do not want that to be an abiding memory and I do not know how long I have got. We talk about the importance of living with our own mortality, and because of losing my dad I am perhaps more proactive in my fathering than I might have been.

My dad was 57 years old when he died, I am 40; there is no guarantee that I will live to be a grandad. I feel my identity as a father quite acutely. I view it as a calling to father my sons and I want to do all I can to help my sons.

- What are the ways that you have been shaped as a man and a father by your dad?

Obviously, there is a genetic and biological link. I notice that in little ways, I find myself sitting on the sofa in the same way as my dad used to sit. My interest in learning and my value of learning is because of him. My interest in exploration, I love to be outdoors, walking and camping. He used to create the family games and I find myself doing that.

- If you were speaking to someone who had lost their dad too soon, what advice would you give them.

My advice would be to see the importance of getting to know God as father and allowing everything they ever thought about father to be rewired to this. One of the most significant things I did was to go through the Gospel of John and every time the word 'father' appeared, I meditated, journalled, and wrote reflections on that. That process made a big impact on me. I would also tell them not to neglect that need within them to be fathered, and to find a healthy shepherd/father man to invest in them.

✴ ✴ ✴

After I conducted these interviews, I read a piece on the playwright Tom Stoppard. Born Tomáš Sträussler, Tom was a year and a half old when he and his family fled Moravia ahead of the Nazis. In January 1942, they fled again, this time from Singapore to escape Japanese troops. Tom's father, a surgeon, did not make it on board with the rest of the family, and the ship he boarded two weeks later sank and he died. Four years later his mother remarried. His stepfather was a British army officer. Tom felt no emotional connection with his stepfather. Then decades later he visited his old home in Moravia – now the Czech Republic. While there he met a woman whose hand his father had stitched when she was a little girl.

> The scar that Tom Stoppard touched on Zaria's hand offers a symbolic compression of flesh and psyche, of the writer's paternal absence, of skin torn and partially mended, of grief owed and loss displaced, of time traversed. Stoppard wrote, "Zaria holds out her hand, which still shows the mark. I touch it. In that moment I am surprised by grief, a small catching-up of all the grief I owe. I have nothing that came from my father, nothing he owned or touched, but here is his trace, a small scar."[7]

Tom Stoppard's experience is a reminder of how deep-seated and complicated grief over the loss of a dad can be. There is some sense of loss, some regret that he is not still around, and some longing to regain something of what has been lost.

It might be something of a generalisation to say that fatherless men and women might be looking for different things in longing for a father. Fatherless men are looking for a hero, someone to look up to, someone who will champion and affirm them. Perhaps that is one of the reasons for the rise of the popularity of superheroes in an age of fatherlessness. Fatherless women are looking for someone to look after them. Maybe that is why some women marry older men or go to church and view pastors as father figures. The common experience here is the search for reassurance. We all need significant figures in our lives. Losing a father leaves an indentation that it is hard to fill.

---

7   Janna Malamud Smith, 'The Scar on The Hand', *Everand*, https://www.everand.com/article/561988171/The-Scar-On-The-Hand accessed 28th December 2023.

Questions:

1) Can you relate to any of the experiences of loss described in this chapter?

2) How might you try to help someone in these circumstances?

3) Why is it important to say a bit more than: 'It's been six months now, shouldn't you be over it?'

4) In what ways can the church be more attuned to these types of loss?

Prayer

Father God, I thank you that you are described as the Father of compassion and the God of all comfort.
I pray for all those who have lost their fathers at a time that seems to be far too early. Lead them to your fatherly care, provide them with mentors and friends who can fill in the cracks of their relational circle.
Father, please show your love to those who have lost their dads, comfort them, help them to be wise in the way they process these losses.
We also pray for those who reach out a hand of friendship to those who have lost their dads, that they might be wise in showing interest and support that serves well but does not lead to dependence, instead promoting a mature and healthy confidence in you our heavenly Father. In Jesus' name. Amen

Action

Think of the people you know whose fathers have died young. Consider ways that you could be supportive to them.

If you are a church leader, think of ways that there can be healthy father figures in the church who are available to mentor those who have lost their own fathers early in life.

'Through the Son we see behind creation into the eternal and essential identity of God. It is as if, through Christ, we step inside the front door of God's home to see who is behind, what he does.' (Michael Reeves)

'You cannot have the Father's gifts if you will not have the Father; for they will trickle through your fingers.' (Helmut Thielicke)

'His sovereignty is one of unlimited power, but also of wisdom and grace. He is both king and Father at the same time.' (Herman Bavinck)

Chapter 10:
God the Father in the biblical story
~ New Testament

If reading the Old Testament on the Fatherhood of God is like looking through a telephoto lens, turning to the New Testament is more like looking through a wide-angle lens. The New Testament is so full of references to God as Father this book would be many times longer if I dealt with all of them. This chapter begins with the distinctive contribution which the Gospels make to our understanding of the Fatherhood of God. In the Gospels we see how God as Father is uniquely revealed in his relationship to the Son. Gradually we will see how we are invited to enjoy access into this relationship through faith in Christ.

Luke's Gospel

Luke is unique among Gospel writers in giving us a glimpse of Jesus as a boy. These thirteen verses in Luke 2:41-52 are the only record we have of Jesus between his birth and the beginning of his public ministry aged 30. The tension in the story is provided by Jesus getting 'lost'. Jeffery observes that:

> It would be a poor parent who would not feel the gravest concern in such a situation, and after a full day's journey back they look for

him everywhere for another day before finding him in the temple, calmly discoursing about Scripture.[1]

The story contains the first words that Jesus speaks in Luke's Gospel:

> "Why were you searching for me?" he asked. "Didn't you know I had to be in my Father's house?" But they did not understand what he was saying to them. (Lk. 2:49-50)

Here is a clear hint that Jesus at the age of 12 was aware of his true identity. Yet the following verse reminds us that Joseph and Mary were still trying to get their heads around the significance of who Jesus really is, and what that meant for the dynamics of their family life. The next scene in Luke's account of the life of Jesus significantly amplifies what it means for Jesus to uniquely know God as his Father.

Baptism

The approving supportive presence of a father at the key moments of life – a school play, sporting events, graduation, wedding – are vital building blocks for a child's sense of their own significance in their father's eyes. The absence of a father at these times sends the message that they are not interested. I have visions of tiny faces looking out at the crowd at a school play or Sports Day, necks craning to catch a sight of dad, like tiny flowers turning their faces to the sun to catch its vibrant rays. No-shows can lead to huge disappointment. John Stark suggests that we are all longing for a father. We all want to be seen. We all want to be noticed. Yet a million 'likes' do not begin to compare with when our Heavenly Father says 'I love you.'[2] The baptism of Jesus was one of the big events in the life of Jesus and the Father shows up in a spectacular way.

---

1 David Lyle Jeffery, *Luke*, (Brazos: Grand Rapids, 2012), p.49-50.
2 John Stark, *The Secret Place of Thunder: Trading our Need to Be Noticed for a Hidden Life with Christ*, (Zondervan: Grand Rapids, 2023), p.22.

> When all the people were being baptized, Jesus was baptized too. And as he was praying, heaven was opened, and the Holy Spirit descended on him in bodily form like a dove. And a voice came from heaven: "You are my Son, whom I love; with you I am well pleased." (Lk. 3:21–22)

It has been noted that prayer is a major feature of Luke's two-part work, Luke and Acts. Jesus and the Church are both shown to pray at key life moments. Here at the baptism of Jesus we see the Fatherhood of God is expressed in attentiveness, affirmation, and approval. The Father's words arise out of the communion of prayer. Jesus models a life of prayer that prioritises intimacy with the Father and which fosters the environment where their intimacy can be experienced. At this moment we capture a snapshot of what a perfect father and son relationship looks like. It is a picture of mutual delight.

Temptation

Fatherless people not only crave significance as they are noticed and affirmed by their fathers, but also desire a sense of security, that there is someone around who is looking out for them. We all need people we can trust who will not let us down. A number of fatherless women have spoken to me about how they feel they have missed out on being held by their fathers, cared for and protected.

After the voice of the Father comes the voice of the tempter. The affirmation of the Father's delight in the Son and the declaration of Jesus' true identity is followed by a dramatic challenge to that identity in the Temptation of Jesus.[3] There is a clear link between the two events. It is interesting that Luke places the genealogy of Jesus between these two events. Luke's version of the genealogy ends with a reference to

---

3   Luke 3:21–22; Luke 4:1–12; see also Matthew 4:1–11, and more briefly Mark 1:12–13

'Adam, the son of God.' The temptations are thus linked with Jesus the true Son and the true man, whose dependence upon and obedience to the Father does not buckle in the face of fierce tests. In each of the three temptations or tests Jesus replies with words drawn from the Old Testament Book of Deuteronomy.[4] Deuteronomy appears to form the biblical baseline for Jesus' identity and behaviour as the Son of the Father. When Jesus quotes the words 'Man shall not live on bread alone' he is not merely saying that human life is more than eating. Seen in the overall context of Deuteronomy 6 – 12, this is not only a smart and highly memorable phrase, but a declaration of the radical dependence Jesus has upon his Father. Jesus trusts the Father for his provision and its timing. He is not giving us another version of 'Live to eat, eat to live!' It is all about who Jesus trusts and how much he trusts him! In response to the three temptations Jesus uses words from the book of Deuteronomy to say in effect:

> Father you have got this:
> Father knows best
> Father deserves my loyalty.

One thing that children look for in their fathers is that they are saying: 'I'll be there for you. I am interested in you. I have your back.' All of these things are evident as Jesus goes through the waters of baptism and the tests in the wilderness.

The heart of Jesus at rest in prayer.

It is a beautiful thing to eavesdrop on an intimate conversation between fathers and their children. They share memories, display intimacy and exercise trust; there is something attractive in the dynamic of their relationships. It reminds me of one of my favourite parts of Luke's Gospel

---

[4] Luke 4:4 (Deuteronomy 8:3); Luke 4:8 (Deuteronomy 6:13) Luke 4:12 (Deuteronomy 6:16)

when he helps us overhear the prayer life of Jesus. Eavesdropping on the prayer life of Jesus we see that the inner core of Jesus is revealed as he prays:

> At that time Jesus, full of joy through the Holy Spirit, said, "I praise you, Father, Lord of heaven and earth, because you have hidden these things from the wise and learned, and revealed them to little children. Yes, Father, for this is what you were pleased to do.
> "All things have been committed to me by my Father. No one knows who the Son is except the Father, and no one knows who the Father is except the Son and those to whom the Son chooses to reveal him." (Lk. 10:21-22)

Tom Wright asks the perceptive question: 'What was it like being Jesus?'[5] This passage begins to move towards an answer of sorts. When we observe human relationships that work well, we talk about chemistry. We say: 'There is a certain chemistry between them.' Isn't that what we see here; a dynamic interplay between the three persons of the Trinity? This is:

> a distinctive insider's perspective ... which nobody is a party to. But just as one may reveal human intimacies, so the Son chooses to share with certain others his own insider's knowledge of the Father. The early Christian boldness in taking over Jesus' own prayer practice of addressing God as *Abba Father*, is a reflection of the revealing activity spoken of here.[6]

It is hardly surprising that immediately after this Luke records the question that the disciples ask Jesus:

---

5 Tom Wright, *Luke for Everyone*, (SPCK: London 2001), p.123.
6 John Nolland, *Luke 9:21-18:34*, (Word: Dallas, 1993), p.577.

One day Jesus was praying in a certain place. When he finished, one of his disciples said to him, "Lord, teach us to pray, just as John taught his disciples." (Lk. 11:1)

Jesus replies with a father-shaped pattern of prayer:

He said to them, "When you pray, say:
" 'Father,
hallowed be your name,
your kingdom come.
Give us each day our daily bread.
Forgive us our sins,
for we also forgive everyone who sins against us.
And lead us not into temptation.' " (Lk. 11:2-4)

It is interesting to compare this brief prayer to the temptations of Jesus. It is almost as if Jesus is consciously articulating in prayer the commitment to his Father that we see displayed in his three-fold answers to the tempter.

This whole incident reminds us that at the heart of the universe there is a relationship, a relationship between a perfect Father and his perfect Son. The astonishing good news of Christianity is that we are invited to enter that transforming friendship as we pray.

The Stories of Jesus

One of the most famous stories that Jesus told was about a Father who had two sons. The story is generally known as *The Parable of the Prodigal Son*, but it is really the story of the *Waiting Father*, whose heart is revealed through the details of this story; the word 'father' is used nine times.

There is one thing about this story that especially ties in with the theme of this book. The parable tells the story of two sons who live at a distance from their father. The younger son has created distance by taking his father for granted, grasping at his resources and getting as far away from home as he could. The elder son lives on the farm, he can see his dad every day yet he too lives at a distance created by his inability to understand the deep well of grace that motivates his father's actions. One son squanders grace, the other does not get his mind around grace at all. It is interesting that it is only the son who ran away who takes the word 'father' on his lips. Only this son 'comes to his senses' and the distance dissolves as he falls into the embrace of his father running towards him. This culturally shocking picture of a running father shows us what the fatherly heart of God looks like. This is fatherhood at its best, revealed to us when we are at our worst.

Often actions like those of the younger son can lead to an irretrievable breakdown of relationship between father and son. Human fathers can so easily turn off the tap of their attention, care and support. God the Father is always looking for the opportunity to dissolve the distance and restore intimacy.

Words from the Cross

When Jesus is on the cross, he speaks seven last statements. In Luke, two of those statements contain the word 'father'. The first of these is Luke 23:34. 'Jesus said, "Father, forgive them, for they do not know what they are doing." ' How remarkable that Jesus on the cross says 'Father forgive'. The heart of Jesus reflects the heartbeat of the Father-love that is depicted in the parable of the Waiting Father. There is always in the heart of God a desire to dissolve the distance and to draw people near.

Luke does not record Jesus' words from the cross that speak about his temporary experience of abandonment, in the so-called cry of dereliction that emerges from the three hours of eerie darkness that envelops Jesus on the cross. However in the second statement containing the word 'father', Luke does record the most tender statement uttered by Jesus as he emerges from the darkness into the light again: 'Jesus called out with a loud voice, "Father, into your hands I commit my spirit." When he had said this, he breathed his last.' (Lk. 23:46)

This transition from the cry of dereliction to a cry of security is so reassuring. The fatherless know something about the darkness and despair of desertion. Here is a reminder that there is hope in the darkness, even in the darkness of the shadow of death itself. Jesus on the cross is like a trapeze artist who has jumped into the dark void, hanging for three hours in that darkness before being caught safely by the strong hands of the Father on the other side.

The Jesus Manifesto

After his resurrection Jesus unveils his agenda for the mission of the Church.

> Then he opened their minds so they could understand the Scriptures. He told them, "This is what is written: The Messiah will suffer and rise from the dead on the third day, and repentance for the forgiveness of sins will be preached in his name to all nations, beginning at Jerusalem. You are witnesses of these things. I am going to send you what my Father has promised; but stay in the city until you have been clothed with power from on high." (Lk. 24:45–49)

The goal of the gospel is that those who live at a distance from God because of their sins might be brought near and experience full forgiveness and the gift that the Father has promised. What is Jesus referring to when he speaks of the promise of the Father? Jesus is speaking of the gift of the Spirit. This gift introduces the Christian believer to a fresh and glorious approach to God the Father that is explored with deep richness by Paul and the other apostles in their letters.

Matthew's Gospel

God's fatherhood revealed by Jesus would have been understood in the first-century as communicating 'both respectful dependence and affectionate intimacy as well as obedience.'[7] Indeed, for Matthew, God's presence is experienced as fatherly.[8]

The theme of the Fatherhood of God is seen throughout Matthew's Gospel, but it is particularly evident in the Sermon on the Mount,[9] where seventeen of the forty-four references to 'father' in this Gospel can be found. The Sermon on the Mount contains the first reference to God as Father in Matthew.[10] There is a particularly dense concentration of Father language in Matthew 6:1-21, which has twelve references to God as Father. This includes the directive of Jesus concerning how we are to address God in prayer. In the words ' "Our Father in heaven" ' (Mt.6:9) the Father is revealed as the central reference point for the whole range of life experienced by the disciples of Jesus.

Thus, throughout the Sermon a major aspect of the teaching is the notion that the disciples of Jesus have God as their heavenly Father. The major function of this "Father" language in the Sermon is to give the disciples a clear and distinct identity as the true children of the God of Israel.[11]

---

7   Craig S. Keener, *The Gospel of Matthew: A Socio-Rhetorical Commentary*, (Grand Rapids: Eerdmans, 2009), p.216.
8   Stephen Barton, in Marianne Maye Thompson, *The promise of the Father: Jesus and God in the New Testament*, (Westminster John Knox: Nashville, 2000), p.106.
9   Mt. 5 – 7.
10 Mt. 5:16. Jonathan Pennington suggests that this signals that references to the Father serve as key summary statements at the conclusion of the main sections of the sermon. The others are found in 5:48 and 7:21. Jonathan Pennington, *The Sermon on the Mount and Human Flourishing*, (Baker: Grand Rapids, 2017), p.99.
11 Jonathan Pennington, *The Sermon on the Mount and Human Flourishing*, p.p. 99-100.

This addresses the deep sense within every human being, especially the fatherless, that we need to know who we are and to whom we belong. In Matthew's Gospel; we are reminded that this is our Father's world, we are his children and we are in his care.

The Fatherhood of God and the Cross

There are approximately 150 instances in the Gospels in which Jesus refers to God as Father. The only exception is in the cry of abandonment from the cross (Mt. 27:46; Mk. 15:34), which is itself a quotation from Psalm 22:1.

> About three in the afternoon Jesus cried out in a loud voice, "*Eli, Eli, lema sabachthani?*" (which means "My God, my God, why have you forsaken me?"). (Mt. 27:46)

Both Matthew and Mark record the words of Jesus in Aramaic. This might suggest that the use of Jesus' heart language is needed to express the depth of the experience that Jesus is enduring.

Some have labelled what is happening here as 'cosmic child abuse'. This is a highly emotive term that might disturb those who have had negative, especially abusive experiences of human fatherhood. It is pastorally insensitive and theologically mistaken to view the crucifixion as the death of an unwilling victim. As John's Gospel reminds us Jesus 'lays down his life' (Jn. 10:17–18). Jesus submits himself to being forsaken so that we might never be. The Son of God is abandoned on the cross, crushed by the weight of our sin, wounded in our place. In his resurrection body he still bears the marks of those wounds. Many fatherless people talk about the incurable wound of fatherlessness. It is a great comfort to know that Jesus was wounded in our place. He was wounded so that we could be healed. Fatherless people also speak about feeling abandoned; for three dark hours Jesus was engulfed by darkness from which arose the sky-piercing cry of dereliction. In the cross the fatherless can identify with a saviour who has experienced the hurt of abandonment. It is a substantial comfort to know that he understands me!

Mark's Gospel

Mark is probably my favourite gospel. The theme of sonship forms the bookends of the major section of his Gospel (1:1 – 15:39). Mark begins with the gospel in a nutshell: 'The beginning of the good news about Jesus the Messiah, the Son of God.' (Mk. 1:1) Mark concludes with the echo of that statement in the affirmation of the Roman Centurion in charge of the detail overseeing the crucifixion of Jesus, 'And when the centurion, who stood there in front of Jesus, saw how he died, he said, "Surely this man was the Son of God!"' (Mk. 15:39)

Although it is the shortest of the four Gospels, Mark often surprises by its unique contributions to the story of Jesus. This includes the only reference in the four Gospels to Jesus addressing the Father as 'Abba Father' (Mk. 14:36). 'We do not have a single example of God being addressed as abba in Judaism, but Jesus always addressed God in this way in his prayers.'[12]

This term, as we shall see, is taken up by Paul in his letters to Rome and Galatia to describe the high point of Christian experience.[13] It is a great privilege given to all believers, but is especially precious to the fatherless, to be able to cry out to God with the very words that Jesus uses in prayer, 'Abba Father'. This is the most astonishing blessing that a human being can experience. I cannot begin to articulate the joy I had when for the first time I addressed a person as Father. That is what I and so many fatherless children have experienced when God the Father has

---

12 Jeremias, *The Prayers of Jesus*, cited in Marianne Maye Thompson, *The promise of the Father: Jesus and God in the New Testament*, p.26.
13 Rom. 8:14–17; Gal. 4:1–7.

dissolved the distance between us by addressing our orphan hearts with his tender, fatherly love.

John's Gospel

Father is the most used term for God in John's Gospel: it appears 120 times. John's emphasis on the Fatherhood of God begins with an intimate veiled reference in the opening verse of his Gospel: 'In the beginning was the Word, and the Word was with God, and the Word was God.' (Jn. 1:1)

The Word is described in his pre-incarnate state as being with or face to face with God. This is a beautiful picture of the intimate relationship that exists between God the Father and God the Son. This relationship is elaborated later in the opening section of John's Gospel.

> The Word became flesh and made his dwelling among us. We have seen his glory, the glory of the one and only Son, who came from the Father, full of grace and truth. (Jn. 1:14)

> No one has ever seen God, but the one and only Son, who is himself God and is in closest relationship with the Father, has made him known. (Jn.1:18)

In both of these verses the relationship between the Father and Son is articulated in the most tender terms. Here is a picture of fatherhood that is attentive, intimate and personal. Here is a Father who is not absent, distant and disengaged.

The opening verses of John's Gospel also remind us that in receiving the gospel we have 'the right to become children of God.' (Jn. 1:12)[14] The

---

14 It is interesting to note that in John's Gospel Jesus is always called Son whereas believers are always called children. There are many children of God but there is only one Son.

coming of Jesus God's Son opens the door for us to become sons and daughters of the living God.

Throughout John's Gospel the words and works of Jesus are closely aligned with the Father. The climax of this identification is seen most fully in the farewell message and final prayer of Jesus recorded in John 13 – 17. In this section Jesus addresses the disciples in all their vulnerability as they come to terms with Jesus leaving them. The disciples are troubled and trembling as they struggle with the prospect of disconnection and absence. Jesus tells the disciples that he will not leave them as 'orphans (metaphorically fatherless); but will come to you.' (Jn. 14:18)

Jesus reassuringly speaks about his Father's house: 'My Father's house has many rooms' (Jn. 14:2). God the Father is not like us with our limited capacity. There is plenty of space in God's house and heart. No believer needs to think that they will be left out of the Father's house. He is the perfect host, who always can find room for more.

For John, the coming of Jesus is the game changer in the way that human beings encounter God. Only the Son can introduce us to the Father; this is what Jesus does: 'No one comes to the Father except through me.' (Jn. 14:6)

> These words express the Fourth Evangelist's unshakable belief that the coming of Jesus, the Word made flesh, decisively altered the relationship between God and humanity. These words affirm that Jesus is the tangible presence of God in the world and that God the Father can be known only through that incarnate presence. Humanity's encounter with Jesus the Son makes possible a new experience of God as Father.[15]

---

15 Gail O'Day, *Gospel of John* (New Interpreter's Bible), (Abingdon: Nashville, 1995), p.743.

It is only the Son who can introduce us to the Father. The climax of this revelation of the Father by the Son is seen in Jesus' interaction with his disciple Philip:

> "If you really know me, you will know my Father as well. From now on, you do know him and have seen him.'
>
> Philip said, "Lord, show us the Father and that will be enough for us.'
>
> Jesus answered: "Don't you know me, Philip, even after I have been among you such a long time? Anyone who has seen me has seen the Father. How can you say, 'Show us the Father'?" (Jn. 14:7-9)

This intimate connection between the Father and the Son ensures that when we come to the Father through Jesus the Son, we come home by entering the Father's House. This talk of the Father's House needs to be read as an expression of the mutual indwelling of God the Father and Jesus that creates the place where believers can belong. Traditionally this reference to the Father's House has been seen exclusively in connection with our heavenly residence. Here the Father's House is seen to be where Jesus is, and Jesus promises that by the Holy Spirit he will be with those who trust him.

> "On that day you will realize that I am in my Father, and you are in me, and I am in you. Whoever has my commands and keeps them is the one who loves me. The one who loves me will be loved by my Father, and I too will love them and show myself to them." (Jn. 14:20-21)
>
> Jesus replied, "Anyone who loves me will obey my teaching. My Father will love them, and we will come to them and make our home with them." (Jn. 14:23)

These verses have always taken my breath away. I am loved by the Father and the Son, and they make their home with me. The words of

Jesus provide trust for our trembling, presence instead of absence, intimacy instead of disconnection. They also introduce us to a dimension of relationship to God as Father that is more than academic. Jesus is describing something that is deeply experiential. Jesus invites us to enter through the front door into God's home.

I remember a visit by a Welsh Preacher to our Monday service at South Wales Bible College, where I was a student. As he was preaching about experiencing God as Father, he introduced us to the Welsh term Cwtch.[16] The preacher explained that this term was difficult to translate into English. Its primary meaning is a tender kiss and a cuddle, its secondary meaning is of a cubby hole or small cupboard, where precious things are stored safely. The combination of these meanings into a cuddle that makes us feel that we are in a safe place may well help us to understand something of what Jesus is promising in John 14. It is one thing to assume we are loved, or to be told that we are loved, it is another thing altogether to feel that we are loved.

The rest of the New Testament

I agree with Blair Linne, when she writes:

> Having God as Father doesn't take away all of the pain of not having our biological dad, but it does help us wrestle through that pain and come out on the other side more dependent upon our unchanging Father.[17]

There is no magic wand that deals with the negative aspects of not having a father or having a negative experience of fatherhood in our lives. In what ways does the gospel begin to fix the Father deficit, how does it fill the hole, heal the wound, replace the missing wires?

---

16 Sounds like 'butch'
17 Blair Linne, *Finding My Father*, p.141.

These questions begin to be answered as our understanding of God's fatherhood develops in the New Testament. There are three factors that help the fatherless become steady on their feet while walking through life.

Firstly, an experience of God as our heavenly Father

Paul picks up Mark's reference to 'Abba Father' in Romans and Galatians to describe the high point of Christian experience: The Spirit of Adoption, as Paul describes him in Romans 8, is a precious lifeline for those who have never had anyone in life that they can call Dad. 'Abba Father'; there is something truly astonishing about being able to use the words that only ever seemed to be appropriate on the lips of Jesus.

> The Spirit you received does not make you slaves, so that you live in fear again; rather, the Spirit you received brought about your adoption to sonship. And by him we cry, "Abba, Father". The Spirit himself testifies with our spirit that we are God's children. Now if we are children, then we are heirs – heirs of God and co-heirs with Christ, if indeed we share in his sufferings in order that we may also share in his glory. (Rom. 8:15-17)

This is a picture of what happens when the generous love of God is poured out in our lives. It is impossible to calculate the liberating impact of taking the word 'father' on our lips for the first time and knowing that we are in contact with someone who loves us with an industrial-strength love that will never let us go. Here is a father who will never abandon us, abuse us, or disappoint us. Such security flows out of the willingness of Father and Son to surrender everything for our sakes.

The eternal Son of God is not spared the full force of abandonment so that we can know that we will never be abandoned. As it says in Romans,

> He who did not spare his own Son, but gave him up for us all – how will he not also, along with him, graciously give us all things? (Rom. 8:32)

Jesus, the dearly loved son, steps into the zone of rejection so that we can be welcomed. Jesus experiences distance from the Father on the cross so that we can be brought near, by his death on the cross.

Being adopted into the family of the living God changes not only our status; it changes us. There is a wonderful transformative quality to this relationship, which we can see in Romans 8:29, 'For those God foreknew he also predestined to be conformed to the image of his Son, that he might be the firstborn among many brothers and sisters.' As Gordon Fee puts it: 'We have been invaded by the living God himself in the person of the Spirit, whose goal is to infect us thoroughly with God's likeness.'[18]

One of the most interesting things about families is how we can become like our fathers and mothers. There is an example of this principle of 'like father like son' that can be seen in a picture of the late Duke of Edinburgh, Prince Philip, that shows him with his left hand in his jacket pocket. He is accompanied by his son, the then Prince of Wales, who also has his left hand in his jacket pocket. Pictures of the present Prince of Wales, William, also show him with his left hand in his jacket pocket. Aspects of our likeness to our fathers are a mixture of nature and nurture. Coming to know God as our Heavenly Father opens up a brand-new dynamic of transformation. This, as we will see next, has a direct impact on our sense of who we are and how we behave. For some fatherless people the idea of being like their earthly father is their worst nightmare; by contrast to be like their heavenly father is beyond their wildest dreams.

---

18 Gordon Fee, 'Rediscovering the Holy Spirit', (*Christianity Today* 17 June 1996), p.22.

Secondly, it is to enter into a new identity

The book of Revelation opens a window on the fresh sense of identity opened up for those who have come to the Father through faith in Jesus.

> Then I looked, and there before me was the Lamb, standing on Mount Zion, and with him 144,000 who had his name and his Father's name written on their foreheads. (Rev. 14:1)

This is a picture of how our new identity is assembled. If a person has grown up with a question mark where the name of their father should be, this sense of bearing the name of someone who has chosen to be our father is so liberating.

John, the author of Revelation, highlights in his first letter something of this sheer wonder of being a child of God:

> See what great love the Father has lavished on us, that we should be called children of God! And that is what we are! The reason the world does not know us is that it did not know him. (1 Jn. 3:1)

'And this is what we are.' Here is the reality of our new identity and status. It might not be recognised on our birth certificate or passport. It might not be acknowledged by people around us, but this is what we are. We know that God has loved us, and we are his children. It does not get better than that, does it? Well, yes it does.

> Dear friends, now we are children of God, and what we will be has not yet been made known. But we know that when Christ appears, we shall be like him, for we shall see him as he is. All who have this hope in him purify themselves, just as he is pure. (1 Jn. 3:2-3)

'Like him.' This is a great work, but it is a work in progress. There is in the Christian life a sense of the *already* and the *not yet*. We are already God's children, but we are not yet all that we are meant to be. Part of that progress comes as we grow in our Christian lives now, but the final transformation will not take place until we see the beautiful one and are transformed into his likeness. This is the great hope of every fatherless heart. It is at the appearance of the Son of God that every tear will be wiped away, every wound healed, and every deficit filled by God's presence. (Rev. 21:4)

Thirdly, a sense of belonging

We have been created to flourish within a range of relationships. We are reminded that the first 'not good' in the Bible is: 'The LORD God said, "It is not good for the man to be alone. I will make a helper suitable for him."' (Gen. 2:18)

God has designed human beings for relationships. Although he is the source of all things for Adam, the man would experience completeness within a relationship with another human being in his life. Like Adam, for whom being alone was overcome by the gift of Eve, I found that, after meeting Jesus, the most important person I have met is my wife. She has unlocked parts of my personality that would not have been expressed if I had lived a solo life. Children and grandchildren have amplified the importance of the blessing of being enriched by meaningful interaction with others. Knowing God as Father means being introduced to community. God is a community of three persons, Father, Son, and Spirit, and we do not fully reflect his image until we live within a community. No man is an island; we all need others. This sense of belonging is enhanced by the community of faith that is the Christian church. There are lots of ways in which the church is described in Scripture: it is a body, bride, temple, house made with living stones, and many more. Perhaps the most relevant image for the fatherless, is God's household.

Three of these references to household in the New Testament deal specifically with the church:

> Consequently, you are no longer foreigners and strangers, but fellow citizens with God's people and also members of his **household**. (Eph.2:19, my emphasis)

> If I am delayed, you will know how people ought to conduct themselves in God's **household**, which is the church of the living God, the pillar and foundation of the truth. (1 Tim. 3:15, my emphasis)

> Since an overseer manages God's **household**, he must be blameless – not overbearing, not quick-tempered, not given to drunkenness, not violent, not pursuing dishonest gain. (Tit. 1:7, my emphasis)

The other references to household in the New Testament letters refer to the homes of Christians, which often doubled up as places where the church met. This means that in the New Testament era, to be invited to church, almost invariably meant being invited into a home.

One of the things that Stanley Griffin (referred to in a previous chapter) taught me was how to experience and appreciate both these meanings of household. Stanley instilled in me the importance of being an active participant in the life of the local church. I remember the text he used so often from Acts, 'They devoted themselves to the apostles' teaching and to fellowship, to the breaking of bread and to prayer.' (Acts 2:42) I heard that text so often as a young Christian that it has shaped my DNA as a Christian and a church leader. Stanley also introduced me to the joy and privilege of being invited into his household. Another text from Acts is pertinent here: 'Every day they continued to meet together in the temple courts. They broke bread in their homes and ate together with glad and sincere hearts.' (Acts 2:46) That text brings together both the commitment to gathering with all God's people and the experience of enjoying table fellowship in people's homes. Finding a place at the table makes people feel welcome and included. When you have grown up feeling that you do not belong anywhere or to anyone, this is a precious gift.

Conclusion

The New Testament shines a bright light on the truth that God is Father. Jesus uniquely reveals to us the nature of God's Fatherhood by showing the richness of his own relationship to the Father. The wonder of the gospel is that Jesus invites us to enter into the experience of that relationship too. One of the joys for the fatherless in this message is that they now know that they have not been left waiting on the doorstep of God the Father's house but have been invited to his table as members of his family.

Questions

1) How does the unique story of Jesus' experience of God the Father help us to see the wonderful dynamics of perfect fatherhood and invite us into a richer experience of God's Fatherhood in our lives?

2) How do we retain the wonder that arises from being adopted into God's family and how do we communicate this reality to those who have tasted the sting of fatherlessness?

3) In what ways does the reality of being part of God's household help us to encourage the church to help the vulnerable feel that they can be part of the family of God?

Prayer

What a privilege it is to be able to call the Creator of the universe: 'Father'. Father God, we delight in knowing you personally.
We thank you for sending your one and only Son to make your fatherly heart known to our orphan hearts.

We thank you for sending your Holy Spirit as the Spirit of Adoption so that we can by your Spirit, cry 'Abba Father.'

We thank you for providing earthly fathers in our homes, and father figures in our churches, giving us safe places that help us grow in our relationship with you.

Father God, make our hearts hospitable to your presence.

Father God, help us to make those who come to you feel at home in your church.

In Jesus' name we pray. Amen

Action

What one thing could you do to foster a greater awareness of God's fatherhood in your life, family, social and church circle?

My friend Jez Field, the pastor of Life Church Seaford is the father of three boys. He has set up a 'Calling all Dads' group in his church. They regularly meet to share on how they were fathered and how they approach fathering. Other churches run 'Who Let the Dads Out' groups on Saturday morning to encourage Dads to spend time with their small children over a cooked breakfast and structured play. Think about what your church could do to encourage a healthy approach to fatherhood.

'We are more than the Facebook family page.'
'Disjunction is at the heart of every family.' (Lem Cisse)

'We might have found ourselves in homes without love, stability or kindness. We might have found ourselves in care for much longer, without the secure attachment that being cradled in a mother's arms brings.

We might have found ourselves in an environment where the man of the house was absent or ever-changing, or where the only male role models were those we glimpsed on the TV.

But the decision made by one couple transformed our lives. And it has meant we've been able to bring up our own children conscious of how terribly precious, and potentially fragile, the security of family life can be.

Instead of carrying a legacy of pain, loss and uncertainty into adult life, with the risk of passing that on to our sons and daughters, we've been given nothing but happy memories of our childhoods and, therefore, a determination to guarantee the same for our own children.' (Michael Gove)

'We know that the whole creation has been groaning as in the pains of childbirth right up to the present time. Not only so, but we ourselves, who have the firstfruits of the Spirit, groan inwardly as we wait eagerly for our adoption to sonship, the redemption of our bodies. For in this hope we were saved. But hope that is seen is no hope at all. Who hopes for what they already have?' (Romans 8:22–24)

'Adoption in Paul has an already/not yet character ... The adoption papers have already been signed and filed and the new relationship has already begun, but the child has not yet gone to live in their new home, which is still under construction.' (Breda Colijn)

Chapter 11 ~ Interview:
Adopted

During one of the Lockdowns in 2020 I finally got around to reading Les Misérables by Victor Hugo. The book is huge and at times it deviates into obscure political and military history. Yet it also has interesting strands concerning fatherlessness.

The first strand relates to a group of aristocratic male students studying in Paris who take working class mistresses, one of whom has a child. When the young men graduate and are about to return to their hometowns they realise that these women have no place in their futures. The women are invited to a special dinner; it looks like a normal event until the young men retire to another room and then leave the place where the dinner has been served. Eventually the young women realise that the young men have paid the bill and left forever. Fantine, the young woman with a child, is left with no means of support and soon is evicted from the home that her young man had funded. The child Cosette is fatherless. Ironically, in the note they left with the women the men say that the women have not known a father or mother but that the young men themselves must return to their fathers and mothers to become respectable citizens and fathers of children!

The next strand comes when the young woman pays a couple to look after Cosette so that she can work. In effect this couple bleed Fantine dry with increasing financial demands but instead of caring for Cosette they neglect her. The couple are supposed to be protecting Cosette, but they mistreated her.

At Fantine's death we see the last strand as her former boss takes it upon himself to care for Cosette. For the first time Cosette has someone in her life who takes on the role of a father. Here is a man who will do anything for this little girl. Cosette has been abandoned, abused, and bereaved but now she is loved, protected and cared for.

Steve Jobs, the Apple founder was adopted, as was actress Marilyn Monroe, South African statesman Nelson Mandela and British politician Michael Gove. Gove writes about one of the sharpest memories of his childhood being when his adoptive mother explained what adoption meant. He recalls the exact words more than four decades later: 'You're different from other children because we chose you. You didn't grow under my heart; you grew in it.'[1] In an interview in *The Times* newspaper he says that he has not sought to connect with his birth mother and knows nothing about his biological father. Gove also said that this does leave lots of unanswered questions:

> "You can't know the balance between the things you adopt from your parents and the things that are a result of genetics," he says. "Most scientists would say that nature is more important than nurture … But I don't think I would be the person that I am, for good or ill, if it hadn't been for my mum and dad and the love they gave and the example they set. Those parts of me that are different, there's a curiosity about, and of course the curiosity is magnified in looking at my own children now."[2]

---

1 https://www.gov.uk/government/speeches/michael-gove-article-in-the-daily-mail-on-adoption
2 https://www.thetimes.co.uk/article/michael-gove-adoption-politics-conservatives-boris-johnson-c5mh3b05j

The biblical character Moses was adopted as a baby by an Egyptian princess but by God's providence had his birth mother as his nursing mother. When we move to the New Testament, the concept of believers being adopted by God is one of the most precious truths in the whole of Scripture.

In his book *The Greatest Secret*, which the author dedicates to his adopted daughter, Krish Kandiah boldly asserts:

> Adoption is arguably the Christian faith's greatest secret. Great in its place in God's plan for the universe. Great in its capacity to reform our life and faith. But also greatly undervalued, greatly underappreciated and greatly underemphasised.[3]

While adoption may be undervalued in today's culture, in the Ancient Greek and Roman world it was viewed as a great privilege; even Emperors like Nero were adopted. For the ancients, adoption was not seen as getting the booby prize that caused embarrassment but like winning the jackpot! Yet it needs to be stressed that ancient adoption was generally a passing on of a legacy to an adult rather than taking on a vulnerable infant.

'The adopted Child has inherited a new family narrative.'[4] This is true both physically and spiritually. An adopted child will have a new set of parents, family network, home, and a whole range of fresh opportunities. This generally means a better life than the child would have experienced in their original context. Yet as we shall see, adoption produces complex reactions in those who are adopted and those who adopt. Krish Kandiah highlights the benefits of spiritual adoption into the family of God: 'According to Paul in Romans 8, the Spirit of Adoption can bring release from the past, encouragement in the present and hope for the future.'[5]

---

3 Krish Kandiah, *The Greatest Secret: How Being God's Adopted Children Changes Everything*, (Hodder and Stoughton: London, 2019), p.20.
4 *Dictionary of Biblical Imagery*, 'Adoption' (p.p. 14–15), p.15
5 Krish Kandiah, *The Greatest Secret:*, p. 47.

The Greek word for adoption appears only five times in the New Testament.[6] Yet it communicates one of the most significant and transformative messages in Scripture. Adoption by Father God is the absolute game changer in the experience of every Christian, but it is particularly special and liberating for those who have been adopted naturally, and who were orphans or fatherless.

The following interview is with a woman I have known since she was in her early 20s. It is only recently that I discovered that she was adopted.[7]

- **When did you have the first inkling that you had been adopted?**

I never had that. There was never a point at which my adopted parents sat me down and said that they had something to tell me. They just raised me in a way that I know that I was adopted. I don't know how they did that, but it was always a part of my life; it was never a secret.

They had one biological child who is five years older than me. My adopted Mum had him and then had an ectopic pregnancy so could not have any more children. She wanted another child; dad didn't really. Mum pushed him into it, so they went ahead and adopted me at 2 months. This meant that I had no baggage.

- **Was there ever a point where you said to them: 'I get that I am adopted, but can you give me a bit more information?'**

I have done that with my adopted mum and have conducted some research. My adopted dad would be very fragile about that. I could never put him into that position. They don't know that I have done some research; I think it would hurt them too much. It is a shame because I would like to speak to them, but they adopted in the 1960s, which is very different from now. Then they separated the child from the biological parents and there was no further contact.

---

6 Rom. 8:15, 23; 9:4; Gal. 4:5 and Eph. 1:5.
7 Interview conducted on Thursday 21st December 2023.

- **How did you feel about that?**

The feelings have changed. As I have got older, I have become more thoughtful about it. The fact that I don't have any blood relatives apart from my own children. Four years ago, my adopted father contracted leukemia. Since he became ill, we have been having six-monthly family get-togethers. I have been sitting in that room surrounded by all the family thinking, I don't really have any blood relationship with any of these people. Yet they have been my family all my life. This has become more and more significant to me. I feel a bit like a spectator as I look around and think 'I don't look a bit like you'.

- **How would you describe the overall experience as a person who has been adopted?**

I felt quite sad for my biological mum. That separation from both my adopted parents and my biological mother is big in my head. Sometimes I don't know what to think about it.

- **Did you have a strong desire to find your birth parents?**

When I had my kids, I began to search. I thought, do I want to get to the end of my life and never know my biological parents? I know names and places; in fact, my biological mum lived about 20 minutes from where I was taken into a family. I found my biological mother's family home and the names of my grandparents but stopped short of trying to make contact. I know my biological father's name and why they were not able to stay together but that is all. I feel sympathy for them because they were pushed apart. They wanted to get married but were not allowed. My biological mother's parents wanted her to have an abortion; that was quite hard to read! My mum chose to be hidden away somewhere till she gave birth to me. Giving birth to my own children I realise how hard it must have been for her.

- Do you imagine anything about them?

I have a photograph of my mum when she is pregnant with me. I don't connect with her when looking at the photo. I think it is odd that she has never tried to get in contact with me.

- What has your experience meant for your sense of identity?

My identity has been shaped by being married to my husband, having kids and grandkids and my identity in Christ. Yet there is sometimes a little bit of a void. There is an unknown thing there, a bit of history. There are some practical implications of this. When I visit the doctors and am asked about family medical history that is all blank space: I have no idea.

- In what ways has the gospel, including its message of adoption, helped you to find significance and security?

I have been adopted once into a loving family and now I have been adopted by Christ. I accept also that my journey in life is what God has wanted me to go through. My parents are not believers and pray that I can put some truth into their lives.

- Some adopted people say that they are special because adopted children have been chosen.

I see it but don't think I feel it. I don't feel that special nor do I feel rejected. I have a wonderful loving family now and can see the journey. The journey that God has put me through is more special than the person. We can use those things. I don't see it as negative.

- How has becoming a mother affected the way you think about your experience and how has your experience helped to shape you as a person?

It is only as you have your own kids that you understand that unconditional love and that bond. I think it made me see how special it was for my adopted mum and dad to accept me as a child into their family. I have discovered through research at Social Services that he said that my adopted dad had a greater bond with me than with his own son. As a mother now it makes me grateful for what they have done for me.

- **What comes into your mind when you hear the word 'father'?**

Father God first. It is an interesting word, I don't see my adopted dad as father, I see him as my dad. He's never had a spiritual input into my life, so I see my heavenly Father as my father. With my biological father, all I have is a name.

- **Do you think that the church gets the implications of being adopted?**

I don't know that they do. I don't think they talk about it. I have only known of one other lady in church, who has had a similar situation. Things can sometimes get mentioned when a preacher is speaking about a difficult subject like divorce or abortion, they say if anyone would like to talk further about this speak to me afterwards. I have never heard that said about adoption.

- **How could it be more sensitive?**

Getting alongside people and getting to know them. There are so many pictures of what family looks like now, so many complex situations. Mother's Day is a strange thing; I feel it every time and on my birthday. I think she must remember that.

- **If you were speaking to a person who has just been told they were adopted, what would you say to them?**

I think it is a privilege. It is not a bad thing, it is amazing.

- Superman was adopted. Do you have any 'superpowers' as a result of your adoption?

More empathy I would say. You can understand people's situations if you have been through them yourself.

- You have done some investigations into your biological parents. How did you go about that?

Social Services. When we moved here, I contacted them. They said that I had to have counselling first. I felt very strong at that time and was in a strong family. They began to send me bits and pieces that they had.

- What were your feelings when you got the first pieces of information?

It was like reading about someone else. It did not seem like my history. It was like reading the story of your own life but not feeling that it was yours. It became clear that my biological mother's parents were quite poor and wanted to save face, so they insisted that I be given up for adoption. She had nowhere else to go. She was a servant in a big house in the countryside.

- Meeting your husband and family was obviously a game changer.

His family are Christians and are very tactile. As I have said, growing up I knew that I was loved but I was never told: 'I love you', and they struggled to hug. So, my husband's family transformed the way that I receive and give love now.

✳ ✳ ✳

As a pastor I have encountered couples who have come to the painful realisation that they were not able to have children of their own. Some of these couples have taken the route of adoption. It has not been pain-free. Some adopted children carry the scars of early childhood traumas. The smallest thing can act as a trigger to remind the adopted person of their story and their pain. A recent episode of Dr Who begins with a baby being left at a church door at the dead of night. The identity of the mother is not revealed but the stark pain of abandonment is palpable. Scenes like this and programmes like *Who do you Think You Are?* and *Long Lost Families*, can be too much to bear. They can stir deep emotions, trigger painful memories and leave an adopted person in tears.

Yet there is great joy in seeing God at work shaping a new narrative for these children. Last Christmas Day I had the joy of seeing a grown-up adopted child and her adoptive mother leading prayers at our Christmas Morning service. I know that there have been some painful episodes and not a few tears in their journey but seeing and hearing them in prayer that morning was a beautiful thing to behold.

Questions

1) Adoption can be viewed as a second-best experience both for the adopted child and the adoptive parents. How can we use the practice of adoption in the ancient world and the biblical concept of adoption to challenge this viewpoint?

2) If you have been adopted, how do you identify and deal with the triggers that bring to mind negative aspects of the past?

3) What can churches do to encourage and support those who take on the vital ministry of fostering and adoption?

Prayer

Father God, thank you for the wonderful blessing of being adopted into your family. We rejoice in the freedom to address you as 'Abba Father'. Help us to live confidently as your beloved children.

We pray for those who have been adopted and for those who have adopted them. Thank you for those who have opened their hearts and homes to children who are not biologically their own. We thank you for those who have used the pain of childlessness to embrace children who are 'parentless'.

We pray for adopted children, remembering the complex feelings of being rejected and chosen. We pray for healing from the sting of rejection. We pray for wisdom to navigate questions of identity. We pray that they will enjoy the love and security of their new homes.

We pray also for those who have taken the step of fostering and adopting vulnerable children. Often these couples are still coping with the trauma of their own childlessness, please comfort them and enable them to embrace these young lives with wisdom and love.

Help churches to know how they can support those who foster and adopt. Make churches places of understanding and welcome.

In Jesus' name. Amen.

Action

If you have been adopted, think of ways that you could use your experience to help others.

Maybe you are a childless couple struggling with what to do next. Have you considered adoption? Adoption is increasingly complicated and involves a long drawn-out selection process that is not for the faint-hearted.

The statistics below indicate that the adoption process is more complicated and takes longer than it ever has.

Perhaps you are a church leader who has members in your congregation that have adopted or fostered children. Think about ways that you can provide support structures for this valuable ministry.

Department of Education Statistics

Here is an article from AdoptionUK, published in 2022, describing the facts at the time regarding adoption:

> Children in England with a plan for adoption are spending longer in the care system before being adopted, according to new government statistics released today. The Department for Education data reveals that these children are spending as long in care as they did in 2015 – two years and three months. The time it takes for a child to be adopted in England has been increasing since 2019, when the amount of time a child spent from entry into care to being adopted was one year and eleven months.
>
> Adoption UK's Chief Executive Emily Frith said: "Once the courts agree that adoption is in the best interests of a child, the sooner they can be matched with a permanent adoptive family, the better. Children in the care system have already experienced so much loss and upheaval. We know that outcomes are better for children who are adopted than for those who grow up in care. Permanence gives children the best chance of a bright future."
>
> The Department for Education figures also show the number of children adopted from care in England has not returned to pre-pandemic levels, increasing by just 2% from last year, when there was a sharp 17% decline in the number of adoptions, largely due to a reduction in court proceedings. There were 2,950 children adopted in the year to 2022, falling from a peak of 5,360 in 2015, since when there has been an overall decline in adoptions. This sits against a backdrop of a rise in the number of children being placed into the care of local authorities – up by 2% this year, to an all-time high of 82,170.
>
> Emily Frith continued: "There is no right or wrong number of adoptions. The crucial thing is that the system must work well for every child with a plan for adoption. Despite a huge amount of

work by the sector in recent years, there is still a lack of confidence within the adoption system. We need to improve judges' confidence that the right families can be found, train social workers to be more confident about making good matches and give adopters confidence that they will be well supported once they adopt. All of us who are involved will have to redouble our efforts."

Other trends include an increase in the number of special guardianship orders granted - up 1% on last year to 3,870. Special guardianship is a court order that places a child with someone other than their parents on a long-term basis. Adoption UK is campaigning for parity of support for Special Guardians, including on access to funded therapy and parental leave allowances.[8]

---

8 https://www.adoptionuk.org/news/children-with-a-plan-for-adoption-are-spending-increasing-time-in-care-before-being-adopted#:~:text=There%20were%202%2C950%20children%20adopted,a-ll%2Dtime%20high%20of%2082%2C170
Published: 17th November 2022. Accessed 17/01/2025

'Well here's a tale, I've not yet told
I was evicted when, I was eight years old
I was shipped off to a dormitory
Full of kids who made no sense to me
And I cried myself to sleep each night
For three straight weeks til' I was dead inside
But I'm not asking for your pity
It's just that fairy tales about fathers make me angry

I was never taught how to deal with this
But I soldier onwards nonetheless
I'm fatherless
And it makes me feel like I'm an alien
Oh Lord, what I wouldn't give
For a caregiver who had care to give
I'm alone and I don't know
How or if to be a man

Look at me now

Vacancy, job vacancy
I need somebody to be the making of me
Someone to take me fishing
You can't blame a grown up kid for wishing
Someone to teach me how to shave
To tut over the mistakes I've made
To offer me some fatherly advice
Some kind of acknowledgement would be nice.' (Frank Turner[1])

'Father is ... the supreme revelation of God, and since the Father is made known to us by Jesus through the Spirit, the full, abundant revelation of God's name is trinitarian: Father, Son, and Holy Spirit.' (Herman Bavinck)

---

1 Song lyrics by Frank Turner, permission granted.

Chapter 12:
Prayer that joins the dots
~ The Christian's response

I love the prayers of the Bible, and often use them as the launching pads of my own prayers. Paul's prayer in Ephesians 3:14–21 is perhaps one of my favourites – I have been praying it for forty years. This meditation looks at how aspects of fatherlessness can be transformed by looking through the lens of this prayer.

Problematical Language

The Archbishop of York, Stephen Cotterill, got into some trouble in the summer of 2023 for suggesting that the biblical language of Father is problematical. To his credit he later clarified that this does not mean we should ditch the language but attach to the label the fullest and richest definition of fatherhood which God the Father perfectly provides.[2]

In the interviews that form interludes in this book I often ask the question: What is the first thing that comes into your mind when you think of the word 'father'? It is an important question. Some people cannot see beyond negative images of fatherhood from their own experience or depictions of fatherhood in our culture. When I think about TV depictions of fatherhood, Homer Simpson is probably the

---

[2] Archbishop of York Presidential Address, York General Synod, 07/07/23.

worst fictional dad ever (as I mentioned in chapter 2)! Often Homer is shown strangling his son Bart. Yet in Season 33 episode 18, after 723 episodes of being a father to Bart, Lisa and Maggie, Homer announces: 'I think I'm finally ready to be a dad!' We might laugh but what we watch can shape our approach to life.

We have seen (in chapter 8) how the actor Mark Strong, whose father walked out on him when he was a baby, says that he does not have a blueprint for being a father. That is the story of millions of people around the world today. How do you build a life, a marriage or a family if you have no blueprint? Here in Paul's prayer we discover that God is the blueprint of fatherhood.

Fatherlessness leaves us rootless

Those who have no earthly father know what it means to be uncertain and anxious about their roots. Yet without Christ we are all spiritually fatherless; we all have the experience of being rootless.[3] The prayer at the end of Ephesians 3 begins with an astonishing line about roots: 'For this reason, I kneel before the Father, from whom every family in heaven and on earth derives its name.' (Eph. 3:14-15)[4]

It is worth noting that kneeling in prayer is comparatively rare in the Bible. The most common posture of biblical prayer is standing or laying down flat on your face. Eugene Peterson reflects on why Paul speaks about praying on his knees.

> While on my knees I cannot run away. I cannot assert myself. I place myself in a position of willed submission, vulnerable to the will of the person before whom I am bowing ... On my knees I am

---

[3] This is something that is explored in Ephesians 2.
[4] 18 out of the 24 references that Paul makes to God the Father in the New Testament arise when during prayer, praise and benediction. It is worth noting the close linguistic link between the Greek words for father (patera) and family (patria), which both form the root of patriarchy.

no longer in a position to flex my muscles, strut or cower, hide in the shadows or show off on stage. I become less so that I can be aware of more – On his knees before the Father, Paul prays.[5]

I like the idea of becoming less in order to be aware of more; that is exactly what we have in this prayer. Paul brings us to the epicentre of who Paul is as a Christian believer. When we pray and address God as Father, we affirm our defining identity. Paul is echoing the first words of the seminal Christian prayer, which in Luke's version begins with the one word: Father. This is the doorway into the world of prayer. The fatherhood of God is the portal through which Paul experiences prayer. This is the foundational relationship of the Christian life. Prayer is the place where we express our Christian identity most clearly. The distinguishing mark of Paul, after as Saul of Tarsus he was stopped in his tracks on the Damascus Road, was 'he is praying.' (Acts 9:11) Paul is in the place where we express our Christian identity most clearly.

Do you see what Paul is doing here? He is rooting the whole of existence, every relationship in heaven and on earth in the reality of God as Father. God is the ideal father, the prototype of all fatherhood, one whose influence extends to the whole cosmos. God's fatherhood is the signal that a better definition of fatherhood exists in the universe. Whenever a human displays the marks of being a good father, they mirror something of God's seminal fatherhood.

This sentence is in some ways the climax of everything in the biblical story. It is the pot of gold at the end of the rainbow; it forms an arc from the call of Abram, as the father of the faithful, to the climatic fulfilment of that call welcoming all nations to be part of the family of God. When God called a man with a name that means father, he is giving us a massive clue concerning what he is planning to do in relationship to the human race. Paul's prayer touches the heart that beats at the

---

[5] Eugene Peterson, *Practice Resurrection: A conversation on growing up in Christ*, (Grand Rapids: Eerdmans, 2010), p.154.

centre of the universe. He is the source, the pattern, the energy, and perfection of all human relationships. Here the rootless find their roots, a firm anchorage point that offers a sense of orientation and stability.

Fatherlessness leaves us powerless

Kneeling before the Father connects us with power that can energise our inner life by the Spirit. Here on our knees, we can experience spiritual reality deep down in our inner life that is not accessible to sight. Our inner self has no resources other than the resources of the Spirit. It is in this place that we can experience daily restoration of our strength that prevents us from being spiritually depleted and unprepared for spiritual growth.

Think about the extent of these resources, 'the riches of his glory', that are available, they are limitless. We simply cannot ask for good things beyond God's power to give them. It is in this place that we can experience daily renewal that keeps us from being spiritually depleted.

Fatherlessness leaves us loveless

Being fatherless starves us of intimacy. Kneeling before the Father connects us with an experience of love that is beyond anything we have experienced before. Ephesians 3:17 contains an extraordinary aspect of this prayer. We are connected to the Spirit's power so that we can experience intimacy with the Son, 'so that Christ may dwell in your hearts through faith.'

Experience that, and you have the whole Christian life! Yet at first sight it is a strange request to make for those who are already believers. We tend to think of Jesus coming into our lives when we become Christians, but this is the only place in the New Testament where the concept is articulated; so, what is being prayed for here? The prayer moves beyond the fact of Christ's presence in our lives to our awareness and experience of that presence at the 'heart' of our lives. In biblical thinking the heart is the centre of personality, the seat of our thoughts, feelings and choices. This seeks for the indwelling of Christ to be more than intellectual or confessional, not merely something we store in our minds or speak about with our lips but something that reshapes our whole lives.

This reality of Christ's presence is experienced by faith. Think of a home that contains the most beautiful treasures, but the owner is blind, and cannot be fully aware of their beauty or the pleasure that their beauty brings. The blind person has to sense the beauty by faith. Perhaps that is what the Apostle Peter describes in his first letter:

> Though you have not seen him, you love him; and even though you do not see him now, you believe in him and are filled with an inexpressible and glorious joy, for you are receiving the end result of your faith, the salvation of your souls. (1 Pet. 1:8–9)[6]

We are to believe, when we pray, that the Christ who dwells in us is a Christ who loves us as no-one else has or ever will. This, says Paul, is like being rooted and grounded in God's industrial-strength love. The strength of this love is spoken of in both biological and architectural terms; it is to be a healthy tree with roots deep in that life-giving love and a structure that is built on the firm foundation of God's solid love.

Fatherlessness leaves you with a reduced life

The fatherless are conscious of what is missing in their lives. Christ opens our lives to the vast dimensions of Christ's love that leads us to the Father.

---

6   See also Jn. 14:21, 23.

> And I pray that you, being rooted and established in love, may have power, together with all the Lord's holy people, to grasp how wide and long and high and deep is the love of Christ. (Eph. 3:17b-18)

Some compare the four dimensions of love with the four points of the compass, conveying the idea of its immensity. Others see a reference to the four points of the cross stretching down from heaven to earth, across the racial and social divides, reaching deep into our lives and stretching from eternity past into eternity future.[7]

This love cannot be fully experienced alone but can only be fully grasped 'together with all the Lord's holy people.' We can only begin to grasp all the contours of God's love as we relate to our fellow believers. As John Stott puts it: 'It needs the whole people of God to understand the whole love of God.'[8] That is of course why the church is such a precious gift to us. The church is God's multi-generational, multi-racial masterpiece that blends people of all shapes, backgrounds, personalities and experiences into one household. It is here that we see the pure light of God's love refracted through the prism of God's new community. Here we witness how the love of God is experienced by old and young, rich and poor, those from functional and dysfunctional families. Here we see those who seem to have charmed lives and those who appear to be crushed under impossible burdens all experiencing God's love. The church is God's masterful arrow of hope for a fragmented world. The arrow points to the reality that God's love is enough for everyone and every situation.

---

7   There is a similar use of these dimensions in relationship to God's mystery in Job 11:8-9.
8   John Stott, *The Message of Ephesians*, (IVP: Leicester, 1979), p.137.

Fatherlessness leaves us running on empty

There is a mysterious known yet unknown quality about this love. What does it mean 'to know this love that surpasses knowledge'? The love of Jesus is like an unbroken circle; you can never get to the end of it! Praying this prayer is like climbing a steep spiral staircase. As we climb the stairs, we begin to get short of breath as we rise higher and higher in our experience of where God's love can take us and where God's love can reach. The climax of this prayer is that we may 'be filled to the measure of all the fullness of God.'

Has anyone ever made a bolder request? It is to be filled with what fills God. What fills God, Father, Son and Holy Spirit if it is not the love of God which dominates this prayer. As John says: 'God is love'. (1 Jn. 4:8, 16) That is what he is essentially. To be filled with God is to be filled with love. Andrew Lincoln suggests that:

> The concern that the readers be filled up to the fullness of God himself can be read as the writer's wish to compensate for any sense of inadequacy and insufficiency on their part.[9]

Isn't that such an appropriate prayer for those who have a father deficit in their lives? Looking at their own image of fatherhood there are so many feelings of what is missing. The love of God begins to address and fill that deficit in ways that are greater than might have been hoped.

How can we be sure in a fatherless world where promises are often empty or undeliverable that God the Father will come through for us? How do we know he can make a difference? People with a father deficit in their lives have lived with a life of disappointment. It seems that they have been waiting for their father to show up forever. Like the child performing in the school show or playing their heart out on the football field, craning their necks to see Dad in the crowd, but he does not show up. Such children grow up coming to realise that adults think that

---

9 Andrew Lincoln, *Ephesians*, (Word: Dallas, 1990), p. 219.

promises are made to be broken! Or perhaps that people want to keep their promises but do not have the resources or resolve to do so. Why should we think it is different with God the Father? The bottom line is that God is both able and willing:

> Now to him who is able to do immeasurably more than all we ask or imagine, according to his power that is at work within us, to him be glory in the church and in Christ Jesus throughout all generations, for ever and ever! Amen. (Eph. 3:20–21)

God our Father is a God of super-abundance. He is the God of more. The Christian counsellor Larry Crabb was asked what he would preach on if he knew he was preaching his last sermon. His answer? 'There's more!' Of course there is more. Sometimes when we get to know a person well there is less and less of them. They are like an onion, we take off layer after layer, only to discover that there is nothing left – except for the tears! Yet the more we get to know God the more and more we discover about the vastness of his riches.

Eugene Peterson tells the story of two of his friends who adopt a five-year-old girl from Haiti after a devastating earthquake that wrecks the island. The couple have two teenage sons who sit with them and the orphan at the dinner table on the first evening. The meal is served and, as happens with teenage boys with hollow legs, all the food soon disappears! The couple become aware that the little girl is becoming anxious at this point; she has experienced unbearable loss and poverty, she has known what it is to go hungry. She is sitting at the table wondering if there will be food on the table tomorrow. The mother takes the girl to the kitchen and shows her the bread bin, which contains three fresh loaves of bread. Then she opens the giant American-style fridge freezer, which is jammed full of food, as is the food pantry next to it. The girl who is used to running on empty needs to know that there is more. It is important for us to take in what Paul is saying.[10]

> God is able to do what we ask in prayer – he is able to do what we fail to ask but can imagine. He is able to do all we can ask or imagine; he is able do more than we can ask or imagine, he is able to do immeasurably more than we can ask or imagine.[11]

What is more, the power of God is at work in us. No wonder the prayer ends with a doxology. 'To God be the glory forever. Amen.'

Questions

1) What key thing about God's fatherhood have you discovered in this meditation? How will it change the way you think about God and yourself?

2) How could you take this prayer and pray it into your life?

3) What does this prayer show about fatherhood in general?

4) When in this letter Paul begins to talk about the role of human fathers, he directly addresses fathers: 'Fathers, do not exasperate your children; instead, bring them up in the training and instruction of the Lord.' (Eph. 6:4) Francis Shaeffer used to say that the best way to translate the word 'exasperate' might be: 'Do not drive your children up the wall.' Fathers are to provide the environment that allows children to flourish. In what way does this reflect God's fatherhood and how can fathers learn to not exasperate their children?

---

10 Eugene Peterson, *Practice Resurrection: A conversation on growing up in Christ*, (Grand Rapids: Eerdmans, 2010), p.159–160.
11 Adapted from John Eadie, *Ephesians*, (London: Griffin, John and Company, 1861), p268–9

Prayer

Father God I know what it is to be rootless, not sure of who I am and where I come from. Thank you that I find my roots in you as my heavenly father. You have reorientated my life, in you I have discovered my true identity.

Father God I know what it is to feel powerless, deflated and devoid of strength. Thank you that you have granted strength that reaches down to my inner life.

Father God I know what it means to be loveless; I am not sure that I know how to feel or receive love. Thank you that you have rooted and grounded me in your love revealed in Jesus.

Father God I know what it is to have a reduced life that often seems to be defined by what is missing. Thank you that you have broadened my horizons to experience the full dimension of your love that reaches every part of me. Thank you for the gift of the church which has given me a multi-coloured, 3D, widescreen version of what you are doing in the lives of others to encourage me to trust that you are lovingly at work in me.

Father God I know what it is to live life running on empty, wondering whether I have enough to keep going. Thank you that you have shown me that with you there is always more. You are enough for me.

Loving God: Father, Son and Holy Spirit you are at work to fill my heart with your love. To God be the Glory. Great things he has done. Amen.

Action

Use the prayer as a launching pad for your own prayers. Sometimes it is good to have something that will prime the pump of our own praying. Learn how to pray this prayer for yourselves and others. Pray through its clauses thinking about how you need to know God at work in your life and the lives of others.

Turn the text of this prayer into a screensaver to greet you each day. Print out a copy and tape it somewhere around the house where you will see it every day.

Think of someone who might be encouraged by this prayer. Send them a copy with a note saying that you are praying it for them.

Chapter 13 ~ Testimony: Turning to our Heavenly Father

Christmas can be a strange and disorientating time for the fatherless. Therefore, I was delighted that when attending my home church a couple of Sundays before Christmas, I had two powerful reminders that God the Father is interested in me and all fatherless people. The first one was that in the morning service the person leading the service specifically prayed for those who are fatherless. It is a simple liturgical step to imagine the circumstances of different people in the congregation and include them in the prayers and preaching. In this way fatherless people, the working class, people of colour feel that they are not invisible but are instead seen, heard and acknowledged.

Then secondly, as part of our evening carol service on the same day, we had the following testimony from one of the young women in our congregation.[1] I listened to Nadia speak with a nod of recognition as she spoke about her own experience of her earthly and heavenly fathers. Her testimony again shows that our expressed or unexpressed longings for a father are only fully satisfied in God.

***

---

1 Permission granted.

I feel very blessed to be able to share my story with you.

I was born in Bulgaria in the early 80s during communist times and grew up in a small town up in the mountains. I am an only child, my parents divorced when I was 5 and my dad remarried and started a new life with his new family, so he wasn't providing any support to my mum. Things were really difficult – financially and emotionally. There was no talk about Jesus in our house until one day my mum, who was a photographer, came home excited because she was employed to take some photos at an Evangelical church. They had some guest speakers from England, and she was asked to photograph the event. She ended up staying for the entire service and that day our lives changed as my mum accepted Jesus in her life and started taking me to church with her. A year or so after, I asked our pastor to baptise me. So, I was baptised in the ice-cold snow-covered river in February 1993, but even though I was just a child – only 8 years old – it wasn't a decision I took lightly. I knew I had met my real Father and it was Jesus who was going to take care of me. And I wasn't wrong.

We were very poor at the time, we lived in very basic council accommodation, the windows were sometimes freezing on the inside in the wintertime and quite often we would forage for food in the woods; my mum just wasn't earning enough to meet our basic needs. One day she told me that she had taken a loan and was moving to live in Israel and that I wasn't going with her. I was placed in the care of my grandparents. They did their best, but they were elderly, uneducated people living on a very minimal pension. My grandparents were not interested in taking me to church, so as I was too young to go by myself, I stopped going.

A few years later, my grandmother was also forced to leave Bulgaria to work abroad. I was then a teenager and it was a really lonely time for me as all my family were leaving one by one. I felt very abandoned and unloved, not good enough and unwanted. I didn't have many friends; I didn't go out as I didn't have anything nice to wear and I was ashamed of my appearance. One day, I was walking aimlessly in town, feeling sad and

I saw our old church – the one my mum used to take me to as a child. I walked in by myself and I broke down in tears. Everyone who remembered me from my childhood was so excited to see me back, so I felt welcome and started attending church again.

At a Sunday service, one morning, I heard our pastor read some words of Jesus

> Ask, and it will be given to you; seek and you will find, knock and it will be opened to you. For everyone who asks receives and the one who seeks finds and to the one who knocks it will be opened.

I took those words in and believed them deeply. So, I started asking.

I never asked for material things, but I did ask God to teach me how to love truly and forgive everyone who wronged me, I asked for wisdom and strength to walk in the right path, I asked God to teach me how to trust Jesus and to build my faith so strong I would never be scared of being by myself again. I said to God, 'Lord, I don't know how, but I do know that you can change my life. I don't see any way out of this lonely, poor existence but you can do anything,' and I asked, 'Lord, if it is your will, please can I be happy.' I prayed every day for what seemed ages, sometimes I would sit on the balcony by myself and pray late into the night.

Then things started happening, the right people started coming to my life, the right connections were made, and doors started opening. Before I knew it, I was leaving Bulgaria – my mum sent me some money to buy a plane ticket and I flew out with a small holdall bag and £20 in my pocket. I was 17 years old and although I was still by myself, I was now in England. I had found a job washing dishes in the kitchen of a café. I slept on a mattress on the living room floor in a friend's flat, but I was able to support myself financially, and was making friends and things were looking better.

At this time, I drifted away from Jesus, although I still prayed from time to time and would give God a thank you nod when things worked out and pray for help when I encountered difficulties. I thought I knew better, and

I would be fine without Jesus. But I wasn't ... of course. I got myself into trouble, anything that the Bible tells us not to do – I did, things I am now highly ashamed of and regret bitterly. I started praying more regularly again, recognising I had turned away from the safety of my heavenly father and I wanted to get close again. I was shown by the Holy Spirit that if I kept going the same way things were not going to end well.

I met Paul and we got married, a few years went by, and we had been trying to start a family for a while, but things were not working out. A lot of dark thoughts entered my head, and I found myself planning an early exit. So, I started praying through a very difficult time. It's a long story but a miracle came called Grayson, my son.

I wanted Grayson to grow up knowing Jesus, so I prayed to God that we find a church. Twenty years had passed since I had last been to church, but I was hoping to find one where we could feel part of a family. Then I met Ellie and Tessa at Ralph's birthday party a couple of years ago and was invited to come along to the Lancing Tab. Again, God answered my prayers and found us a church where Grayson can grow up learning about Jesus and we could feel part of a church family.

Then God added another miracle to our family, Dolly.

God pulled me through feelings of abandonment, desperation, loneliness, depression, freed me from addictions, brought me back to my senses when I was in deep sin; provided for my physical and emotional needs when my parents weren't there; gave me a family of my own when it wasn't looking at all possible, a house and material possessions even though I never asked for them and they were never a focus for me; gave me my dream job of training, developing and mentoring others when I had no education or qualifications to do that whatsoever. He also pulled me out of darkness and made me feel loved at a time when no one else did. He taught me how to forgive and trust him with my life, and he also made me feel truly happy – just as I asked him to do all those years ago.

Last year my biological father passed away. I felt sad obviously and attended the funeral, but I didn't feel like I lost my father then. I feel like my real father is very much alive and is holding my hand every step of the way. I don't know why I had to go through what I went through, but I trust Jesus that it was all for my good. Even If the reason for having all these experiences was just so that I can share it all today to God's glory."

Questions

1) Did you notice how many links were in the chain that led to Nadia coming to a settled place of confidence in Christ?

2) How can we be alert to the opportunities that arise for us to be strategic links in the chain that leads people to know their true North in God: Father, Son and Holy Spirit?

Prayer

Father God, thank you that you are the Father of the fatherless.
We are not invisible to you; you see us and know our needs before we ask you. Draw people today to you.
We pray that there will be many more stories of those who feel abandoned experiencing fresh hope in you.
Help all those who lead services or preach to be sensitive to those who have a huge hole in their lives because they are fatherless.
Lord Jesus, wounded for us on the cross, we thank you that by your grace and tender mercy you soothe our sorrows, heal our wounds, and drive away our fear.
Spirit of God, create and keep alive in us the joyful delight and security of being able to say 'Abba Father'. Amen

Action

If you are involved in leading or preaching in your church services: How you could be more sensitive to the range of people who attend? How can you communicate this attentiveness in your leading and preaching?

'My home has an absent space, a ghost in our pictures, there is a missing puzzle piece I can never find.

...

He was never in my midst. He was a mist and I missed him.

...

Fatherlessness is a machete at the neck of the nuclear family. Seeking to separate the head from the body. Giver from the receiver. But Fathers we need you. You are important.' (Blair Linne, 'Finding My Father')[1]

'The real theological issue is not whether God can be experienced in a fatherly way but whether God can be trusted to fulfill the promises and obligations that the Bible ascribes to him as father. Looking to God as Father, that's always a stance of faith and hope.' (Marianne Meye Thompson)

---

1   https://www.youtube.com/watch?v=hx4DS5-NGaE

Conclusion:
Knowing our Heavenly Father

As I draw this book to a conclusion there are a few loose ends that I want to address. It has not been possible to deal with every biblical text related to fatherlessness and the fatherhood of God. There would be scope for a book twice the size of this one to cover only the New Testament material. I am also aware that much more could have been said about the cultural and social analysis of issues raised in these pages. My main focus has been to give a flavour of what it feels like to be fatherless and provide some biblical pointers to how the matter can be addressed by the church. Whatever our own experience may be, as Christians we know perfect spiritual fatherhood in God our Heavenly Father, who also teaches us to care for those who are humanly fatherless.

A big thank you to those fathers without whom we would all be less

This is a good point at which to give a shout out to all the good dads that are out there. Fathers, we need you. Thank you for who you are and what you do. This book has intentionally concentrated on the father deficit in contemporary society, but it is important to acknowledge that the situation would be far worse without you. You have been there for your children, you have shown them love, you have cared for them, trained them and championed them. You have allowed them to dribble over the shoulder of your brand new lambswool sweater, you have got out of bed early to play with Lego or to watch yet another episode of *Peppa Pig*. You have been to the school play, stood on the touchline at the football in the pouring rain; you have been the breakfast maker, packed lunch filler, taxi driver, and storyteller. You have taught us how to tie our shoes, ride our bikes and how to relate to other children, adults and God. Your presence has been as predictable as your dad jokes. We have laughed together, cried together, eaten together, played together, prayed together. You have given us your time (that is, of course, how we spell the word 'love'), you have listened to us, and you have taken us seriously. My friend Richard Underwood said of his father:

> Whenever I think of my Dad, I smile and thank God for a man who taught me so many good things – including how to prize the gospel, work hard, see the best in people, and, above all, love my wife and respect women.

At their best, good fathers point beyond themselves to the perfect father we all long for. Thanks dads! Andy Constable of 20schemes in Scotland sums it up well:

> My own dad was a great father, a godly man. Loved us well, very present in the home, worked hard, and provided for us. My father was a reflection of my Heavenly Father.[2]

In this book I have tried to funnel my emotions, experiences and observations through the lens of Scripture. If there are ways to navigate the choppy waters of fatherlessness and find a way through to better relationships, Scripture itself must be allowed to speak with clarity to this situation. This is what I have attempted to do in this book. I would

---

2 In conversation.

like to conclude by looking at two key verses from the Letter of James that underline what I have written. These two verses remind us of what we have discovered about the character of God the Father and underline the priority that God the Father gives to the care of the fatherless.

Manifesto on Fatherlessness

James 1:27 is a verse that would not look out of place in the Old Testament. Perhaps that is one of the reasons that Martin Luther had his struggles with the letter to James. At first sight it and many other statements in this letter don't appear to have the full gospel ring. Yet James wants to remind us that being a Christian is not merely about what we believe, it is also about how we behave. The great thing about this statement is that it does form a brilliant bookend with the material in the Old Testament that affirms God the Father's deep commitment to the fatherless.

It reminds us that there is a beautiful continuity between the God of the Old Testament and the God of the New. This statement reminds us of what God is looking for in the practical outworking of our faith in him as our Heavenly Father. The Father accepts our religious observance as pure and faultless when we reflect his fatherly character and care in our lives of compassion and service. Godly people are both holy and helpful. Pure and practical. Heavenly minded and of earthly use.

James is defining what the real deal is for Christian practice.

> Religion that God our Father accepts as pure and faultless is this: to look after orphans and widows in their distress and to keep oneself from being polluted by the world. (Jas. 1:27)

If this text, with its echoes of Old Testament ethics, sounds to your ears like an unusual addition to a New Testament letter; how did it get here? Scot McKnight in his translation of the New Testament, *The Second Testament*, makes the helpful suggestion:

> The author is most likely the "brother" of Yēsous. If so, the expression of 1:27 ("orphans and widows") opens a door into life in the home of Yakōbos [James] in Nazara [Nazareth].³

They say that 'It takes one to know one.' I think it is true that those who have in one way or another experienced fatherlessness, actual or metaphorical, tend to be able to speak in a language that other fatherless people can understand. Opening a door onto the home of Mary, James, Jude and Jesus after the loss of Joseph reminds us that at some stage this family was one of orphans and widows. Joseph does not make an appearance in the Gospels after Matthew 2 and Luke 2. Assuming that McKnight is right we can conclude that Jesus and his half-brothers understand the experience of human fatherlessness from the inside. This creates a fascinating backdrop to James' directive and reminds us of the breadth and depth of Jesus' identification with us in our humanity. James 1:27 ensures that we do not place our concern about widows and orphans on the back burner. When we read the whole New Testament, we see that Christianity is about more than this, yet it must never be about less. Genuine Christianity should always be seeking to create a space for those who have no place, provide a welcome to those who have been overlooked, and offer love to those who have been denied love.

It is worth noting the word James uses to describe the situation of widows and orphans: he describes it as 'distress'. This reminds us of the considerable trauma experienced by those who lack a significant and reliable father figure in their lives. I have tried not to make this book simply about statistics but the statistics for fatherlessness in the United Kingdom are devastating. Approximately one in two boys aged 15 are not living with both parents, of which 90% aren't living with their father.⁴ Clearly this is not a marginal issue. Yet when was the last time you heard

---

3 Scot McKnight, *The Second Testament*, (IVP: Downers Grove 2023), p.256.
4 https://www.chapter2.org.uk/fdc

a sermon about fatherlessness? When the fatherless step into a church they want to hear and see demonstrated a statement that the church is there for them, that they are part of the agenda. This will not occur automatically in the church, it requires intentionality on the part of church leaders, who need to develop an ethos and strategy that serves the needs of the fatherless. Often it is not until the church is presented with an obvious influx of people who need particular attention that any action is taken. We see this in the crisis of care for widows in Acts 6:1–7. The neglect of one group in the church was a scandal that threatened the well-being of the church and the credibility of its witness. Such problems arise in the church when certain groups within the church are invisible. That is, they are present but not acknowledged. It is not until the church begins to detect its blind spots and learns to really see people that are different that it will be able to make progress in including and caring for everyone in the church. The way that the Apostles acted swiftly and decisively to defuse the problem and create an ethos, strategy and mechanism to deal with it is a model for church leaders in similar situations.

Another of the three references to God as Father in James reminds us that what we believe about God should transfer into how we view people.

> With the tongue we praise our Lord and **Father**, and with it we curse human beings, who have been made in God's likeness. (Jas. 3:9, my emphasis)

We cannot fool ourselves that we are praising God if we treat people like trash.

I read the obituary of Adrian Street, a former miner turned flamboyant wrestler who recently died. He was speaking about the return of his father from the war in the Far East. I was struck by how he described his father:

> I didn't get a knight in shining armour, the hero I thought I was going to get, and a dad that was going to love me. All I got was a Bible-bashing bigoted bully who never said a kind word to me in his life.[5]

It is difficult to make sense of our lives when those who have the label father do not display the characteristics of true fatherhood. It creates distress, confusion and trauma.

This is also a good point to give a shout out to single mothers, who have often been cast as 'shameless Jezebels sponging off the state and contributing to the breakdown of family life'. There might be some women who fall into that generalised category but there are many who valiantly hold the fort when their men go AWOL. Being both Mum and Dad, breadwinner, cook, cleaner and guide rolled into one is a massive achievement. Many single mothers, whether unmarried, divorced or widowed, are the one fixed point in their children's lives. Take Mary as a case in point. She brings up Jesus, is the catalyst for his first sign in John's Gospel, acts as a mother figure for John the Apostle and is a founder member of the church in Jerusalem. Talk about multi-tasking! Thanks, mums.

Motivation for tackling fatherlessness

It is important to see how what James says about widows and orphans is related to God as Father. We have already seen how James points us to the constancy of God the Father. James bases his teaching about fatherlessness on the foundation of a remarkable truth about God as Father:

---

5 *The Times Online*, Wednesday 9th August 2023. Maybe Street was a bit harsh about his father; navigating the traumas of the war in the Far East and re-entry into normal family life was a huge challenge.

> Every good and perfect gift is from above, coming down from the Father of the heavenly lights, who does not change like shifting shadows. (Jas. 1:17)

This is an antidote to the nightmare of the fatherless. Those with absent or abusive fathers simply do not know where they are with their father. One minute they are there and then they are gone. One moment they are generous and then they are cruel. That rollercoaster ride of contrasting experiences and emotions is exhausting. God the Father is different. As Amy Peeler reminds us: 'James says that there is not even one variation or turning to the dark side in God.'[6]

James 1:17 tells me three important things about God that speak to the father deficit in human society:

1. Fatherlessness takes people to a bad place *but*
   God our Father is good and what he sends us is good.
2. Fatherlessness takes us to a dark place *but*
   God our Father is the source of light.
3. Fatherlessness takes us to an unstable place *but*
   God our Father is unchanging in his faithfulness.

What the fatherless and all of us need is a sense that we can know a Father who is trustworthy.

> To trust in the one who is known through the Scriptures and through the words of Jesus as Father is to trust in God as one who is and will be faithful.[7]

---

[6] Amy Peeler, *Women and The Gender of God*, (Eerdmans: Grand Rapids, 2022), p.206.
[7] Marianne Meye Thompson, *The Promise of the Father*: p.85.

Make you feel my love[8]

Fatherlessness not only creates uncertainty, it also breeds anxiety about whether a person will ever be able to receive love. When our trust is betrayed by an earthly father it is difficult to trust any father figure or person in authority. CS Lewis talked about how if we want to prevent our heart from being broken, we can lock it away in a box, then it will never be broken, but neither will it ever feel love. What are we to do with this reluctance to open the gate of our heart for fear that it might lead to disappointment and heartbreak? Two intriguing statements made by Jesus' other half-brother Jude might help us with this.

> Jude, a servant of Jesus Christ and a brother of James, to those who have been called, **who are loved in God the Father and kept for Jesus Christ**: Mercy, peace and **love** be yours in abundance. (Jude 1-2, my emphasis)

> But you, dear friends, by building yourselves up in your most holy faith and praying in the Holy Spirit, **keep yourselves in God's love** as you wait for the mercy of our Lord Jesus Christ to bring you to eternal life. (Jude 20-21, my emphasis)

At first sight these statements look like a contradiction in terms, but in fact they can be some of the most encouraging statements for those who struggle with receiving love. The first statement reminds us that we are held with a firm grip by God's fatherly love in Christ. The second statement encourages us to live experientially in that love. One of the most important things about the Christian life is knowing that we are loved by God as a fact and growing in an awareness of that fact in our experience. This is not an automatic thing. We need to keep preaching

---

8 This heading, which uses the title of a Bob Dylan song, is prompted by Julian Hardyman, who on reading my book *God is in the House*, expressed surprise that I had made no reference to Bob Dylan!

the gospel to ourselves. It is the truth that sets us free, for sure, but it is truth applied that helps us travel lightly in the assurance of that truth. Sometimes it takes a small child to remind us of the dynamics of this process. A grandchild might say to me: 'Pops, I love you,' adding for effect, 'Pops, I really really love you!'

Preach the gospel to your heart. Reckon on God's fatherly love for you. Receive that love for you. God, Father, Son and Holy Spirit unite to say: 'we really love you.'

> The grace of our Lord Jesus Christ, and the love of God, and the fellowship of the Holy Spirit be with you all. (2 Cor. 13:14)

Questions

1) If there was one thing that you could take from this book that would help you to know God the Father better, what would it be?

2) If there was one practical step you could take as a result of reading this book what would it be?

3) The main question is not 'How can we hide our wounds?' but 'How can we put our woundedness in the service of others?' (Henri Nouwen) If you are a fatherless person how can you use your woundedness in the service of others?

4) What might it look like in your life and church to take seriously the words of James 1:27?

Prayer

We believe in God the Father Almighty. Father God, thank you that you are Father all the way down to your core.
The one who is and was and is to come, the Almighty.
In an unstable world you are my stability.
In a world of shaken foundations, you are my rock.
In a world that lets us down, your faithfulness is new every morning.

There is no dark side to you, O Lord. You are pure, undimmed constant light.

We thank you that in Jesus you know something about fatherlessness from the inside.

Lord, we come to you with confidence because you have never failed us. Help us to grasp the wonder of your fatherly care and to reflect that care in serving those who need to know you and the depth of your love. We pray this in Jesus' name. Amen.

Action

If you are a fatherless person, reflect on how you respond personally to what you have read in this book. Have you identified areas in your life that continue to be blighted by a father deficit? Do you need to talk about it with someone? Do you need counselling? Do you need help to apply the gospel to your heart?

For all readers: use the interview interludes to reflect on the many ways that people can be fatherless. Think about how you could be involved in serving the fatherless.

Acknowledgements

I am grateful for the opportunity to acknowledge my debt to so many people who have contributed to the production of this book.

Thanks to Judith Dennis, who has again read through all the chapters checking my spelling and looking out for missing or misplaced commas, semi-colons and apostrophes! Thanks also to Judith for compiling the bibliography.

Thanks to Helen Gray and the team at Grace Publications for getting this book over the line. Helen has kindly and methodically helped me through all the editing and pre-production stages for the book.

Thanks to Will Cockram, the pastor of Cuckfield Baptist Church for suggesting that I approach Grace Publications to produce this book. Thanks also to the church in Cuckfield for listening to four sermons on fatherlessness that informed one of the chapters in this book and welcoming Anne and I among you for 2024.

Thanks to staff and scholars at Tyndale House in Cambridge for a stimulating week in January 2022 where I was able to research and sketch the sections of this book that deal with fathers and Father God in the Old and New Testament.

Thanks to John Kirkby and the anonymous interviewees that shared their stories with me (sometimes with pain and through tears). Thanks too for all the people who have spoken to me about their father issues

Thanks to the singer Frank Turner for permission to quote part of his song 'Fatherless', and to Connor Allen, Children's Laureate Wales 2021–2023, for permission to use part of a conversation I had with him.

Thanks to John Stevens, the National Director of the Fellowship of Independent Evangelical Churches (FIEC) for his gracious and moving foreword.

Thanks to all those who have taught me about the fatherhood of God and those who have modelled what it means to be a good father. Thanks also to those who have been father figures for me as I have navigated my way through life.

Thanks to the churches in Lowestoft and Lancing where as a pastor I learned many of the insights that I share in this book.

As always, thanks to my wife Anne and my family, who have opened a safe place in my life where I know I am loved.

Finally, I am thankful to my heavenly father, who knows my needs before I ask him. At last, I have someone who I can approach and call, 'Father'. He knows me and loves me; I know him and love him. I have not seen the face of my earthly father, but I will see my heavenly father's face.

It does not get much better than that!

Bibliography

Adoption UK, *Children with a plan for adoption ar spending increasing time in care before being adopted*, [article], 17 November 2022, Adoption UK, https://www.adoptionuk.org/news/children-with-a-plan-for-adoption-are-spending-increasing-time-in-care-before-being-adopted#:~:text=There%20were%202%2C950%20children%20adopted,all%2Dtime%20high%20of%2082%2C170

Beck, John A., *Zondervan dictionary of biblical imagery*, Zondervan, Grand Rapids, 2011

Beckham, Hannah, 'Cutting ties with my father was the best thing I ever did', *iPaper*, (9 January 2023)

Bennet, Nel, *A Chance to be Sorry: Forgiving those who are not sorry*, Nel Bennet 2018

Beeswing, Richard T, *Losing my way, finding my voice, 1967-1975*, Algonquin Books, London, 2022

Biography.com, Anni-Frid Lyngstad, [biog]. [n.d.] https://www.biography.com/musician/anni-frid-lyngstad, accessed 5 October 2021

Bono, *Surrender: 40 songs, one story*, Hutchinson-Heinemann, London, 2022

Bos, Rein, *We have heard that God is with you: preaching the Old Testament*, Eerdmans, Grand Rapids, 2008

Botterwick, G. Johannes & Ringgren, Helmer (eds), *Theological Dictionary of the Old Testament, Vol. 1*, trans. John T. Willis, Eerdmans, Grand Rapids, 1974

Bowser, Clive, *Life in the Son: exploring participation and union with Christ in John's gospel and letters*, (New Studies in Biblical Theology), IVP, Leicester, 2023

Bowser, Clive, *One, being united to Jesus changes everything*, Union Publishing, Bridgend, 2023

Boyne, John, *A history of loneliness*, Transworld Publishers, London 2015 [Kindle edition, location 2024]

Buechner, Frederick, *Peculiar treasures: a biblical Who's Who*, Harper Collins, New York, 1979

Callahan, Allen, *Joseph: story and history of interpretation*, (New Interpreter's Dictionary, 3), Abingdon, Nashville, 2008

Calvin, John, *Institutes of the Christian religion*, ed, John T. McNeill, trans. Ford Lewis Battles, The Westminster Press, Philadelphia, 1960

Chen, Diane G. *God as Father in Luke-Acts* (Studies in Biblical Literature:92) Peter Lang Verlag, New York, 2006

Church of England, *Presidential address of the Archbishop of York to the General Synod*, [address], 7 July 2023, Church of England, https://www.churchofengland.org/media/press-releases/presidential-address-synod-archbishop-york

Churchill, Andrew R. *Walking with destiny*, Allen Lane, London, 2018

Collier, Winn, *A burning in my bones: the authorised biography of Eugene H. Peterson*, Authentic, London, 2021

Cook, Stephen, *Reading Deuteronomy: a literary and theological commentary*, Smyth and Helwys, Macon

Craigie, P. C., *Deuteronomy*, Eerdmans, Grand Rapids, 1976

Cruddas, John, *A century of Labour*, Polity, London, 2024

Davidson, Robert, *A commentary on the Psalms: the vanity of worship*, Eerdmans, Grand Rapids, 1998

Davis, Ellen, *Getting involved with God: rediscovering the Old Testament*, Cowley, Cambridge, Massachusetts, 2001

Eadie, John, *Ephesians*, Griffin, John and Company, London, 1861

Evans, Mary, *Judges and Ruth* (Tyndale Old Testament Commentaries), IVP, Leicester, 2017 [Kindle edition, location 2268]

Fee, Gordon, 'Rediscovering the Holy Spirit', *Christianity Today*, (17 June 1996)

Goldingay, John, *Numbers and Deuteronomy for everyone*, Westminster John Knox, Nashville, 2010

Gove, Michael, [*The story of my adoption*], [article], 7 November 2011, Daily Mail, https://www.gov.uk/government/speeches/michael-gove-article-in-the-daily-mail-on-adoption

Gove, Michael, *When you are adopted, you want to prove yourself*, [article], [n.d.], The Times, https://www.thetimes.co.uk/article/michael-gove-adoption-politics-conservatives-boris-johnson-c5mh3b05j

Jeffery, David Lyle, *Luke*, Brazos, Grand Rapids, 2012

Jeremias, *The prayers of Jesus*, in Thompson, Marianne M *The promise of the Father: Jesus and God in the New Testament*, Westminster John Knox, Nashville, 2000

Junod, Tom, 'Can you say hero?', *Esquire*, (7 April, 2017)

Kandiah, Krish, *The greatest secret: how being God's adopted children changes everything*, Hodder & Stoughton, London, 2019

Keener, Craig S, *The gospel of Matthew: a socio-rhetorical commentary*, Eerdmans, Grand Rapids, 2009

Keller, Timothy *Judges for you*, The Good Book Company, London, 2013

Keller, Timothy, *My rock, my refuge*, Hodder & Stoughton, London, 2015

Kidner, Derek, *Psalms 1-72*, IVP, Leicester, 1973

Lawson, Mark, 'Cary Grant's whole life was a civil war: the TV drama unmasking Hollywood's permatanned icon, *The Guardian*, (13 November 2023)

Lincoln, Andrew, *Ephesians*, Word, Dallas, 1990

Linne, Blair, *Finding my father: how the gospel heals the pain of fatherlessness*, The Good Book Company, London, 2021

Linne, Blair, *Finding my father*, [video], [n.d.], https://www.youtube.com/watch?v=hx4DS5-NGaE

Long, Thomas, G. *Matthew*, John Knox, Westminster, Louisville. 1997

Lyngstad, Anna-Frid, [biog] [n.d.] ABBA, https://abbasite.com/people/anni-frid-lyngstad, accessed 5 October 2021

McConnell, Mez, 'Abuse and the gospel' in *Sermons from the Schemes*, Grace Publications, London, 2023

McConnell, Mez, *The creaking on the stairs: finding faith in God through childhood abuse*, Christian Focus, Fearn, 2019

McFadyen, Alistair, *Bound to sin: abuse, Holocaust, and the Christian doctrine of sin*, Cambridge University Press, Cambridge, 2000

McKnight, Scot, *The second testament*, IVP, Downers Grove, 2023

Millar, J, Gary, *Now choose life: theology and ethics in Deuteronomy*, Apollos, 1998

Miller, Donald, *Father fiction chapters for a fatherless generation*, Howard Books, Brentwood, 2019

Moyle, Marsh, *Rumours of better country: searching for trust and community in a time of moral outrage*, IVP, Leicester, 2023

Nolland, John, *Luke 9:21-18:34*, Word, Dallas, 1993

O'Day, Gail, *Gospel of John*, (New Interpreter's Bible), Abingdon, Nashville, 1995

ONS, Census 2021. People, population and community: births, deaths and marriages, [article], https://www.ons.gov.uk/peoplepopulationandcommunity/

birthsdeathsandmarriages/families/articles/familiesinenglandandwales/census2021

Packer, J.I., *Knowing God*, InterVarsity Press, Downers Grove IL, 1973

Peeler, Amy, *Women and the gender of God*, Eerdmans, Grand Rapids, 2022

Pennington, Jonathan, *The sermon on the mount and human flourishing*, Baker, Grand Rapids, 2017

Peterson, Eugene, *Practice resurrection: a conversation on growing up in Christ*, Eerdmans, Grand Rapids, 2010

Peterson, Eugene, *Praying the Psalms*, Zondervan, San Francisco, 1993

Peterson, Eugene, *Praying with Jesus*, Zondervan, San Francisco, 1993

Petrenko, Ester, *Ephesians*, (Central and Eastern European Bible Commentary, ed. Corneliu Constantineanu), Langham Publishing, Carlisle, 2023

Philips, J B, *Your God is too small*, Epworth Press, London, 1952

Pierson, Lance, *In the steps of Timothy*, IVP, Leicester, 1995

Redwood, Christine, *Preaching Old Testament narrative to Australian congregations*, ed. Ian Hussey, Morling Press, Macquarie Park NSW, 2019

Robinson, Marilynne, *Reading Genesis*, Virago, London, 2024

Rogers, Richard, *A commentary on Judges*, Banner of Truth, Edinburgh, 1983

Sasson, Jack M. *Judges 1-12*, Yale University Press, New Haven, 2014

Smith, James K A, *On the road with Augustine: a real world spirituality for restless hearts*, Brazos, Grand Rapids, 2019

Smith, James K A, *How to inhabit time*, Brazos, Grand Rapids, 2022

Smith, Janna Malamud, 'The scar on the hand' The American Scholar, (1 March 2022)   https://www.everand.com/article/561988171/The-Scar-On-The-Hand accessed 28th December 2023.

Sowers. John, 'Filling the Dad Gap' *Christianity Today* (January 2011)

Stark, John, *The secret place of thunder: trading our need to be notices for a hidden life with Christ*, Zondervan, Grand Rapids, 2023

Stott, John, *Issues facing Christians today*, 4th ed., Hodder, London, 2006

Stott, John, *The message of Ephesians*, IVP, Leicester, 1979

The Guardian, *Vicar who cannot forgive tube bombers quits pulpit*, [article], 7 July 2006, https://www.theguardian.com/uk/2006/mar/07/religion.july7, accessed 15 January 2024

The Spectator, Rod Liddle is right about black boys and absent dads, [feature], [n.d.], The Spectator, accessed 6 January 2024 https://www.spectator.co.uk/article/rod-liddle-is-right-about-black-boys-and-absent-dads/,

Theroux, Louis, *Stormzy*, (Louis Theroux Interviews Series 1, episode 1) [broadcast], [n.d], BBC, https://www.bbc.co.uk/iplayer/episode/m001djpl/louis-theroux-interviews-series-1-1-stormzy, accessed 6 January 2024

Thompson, John I, *Reading the Bible with the dead: what can you learn from the history of exegesis that you can't learn from exegesis alone?*, Eerdmans, Grand Rapids, 2007

Thompson, Marianne M, *The promise of the Father: Jesus and God in the New Testament*, Westminster John Knox, Nashville, 2000

Tozer, A W, *The knowledge of the holy*, Alliance Publications, Peabody, Massachusetts, 1961

Trible, Phyllis, *Texts of terror*, Fortress Press, Minneapolis, 1982

Turner, Frank, On reconciling with his trans parent Miranda [who] is a really nice person my dad wasnt, [feature], [November 2021], The Guardian, https://www.theguardian.com/music/2021/nov/25/frank-turner-on-reconciling-with-his-trans-parent-miranda-is-a-really-nice-person-my-dad-wasn't, accessed 22 November 2021

Webb, Barry G, *The book of Judges*, (TNICOT), Eerdmans, Grand Rapids, 2012

Whyte, Alexander, *Bible characters: the Old Testament*, Oliphants, London

Wright, Tom, *Luke for everyone*, SPCK, London, 2001

Also available

A free companion resource aimed at those who have pastoral and preaching responsibilities

What are the issues that may affect how we preach about fatherlessness or the fatherhood of God? What are some helpful guidelines for preaching sensitively on this issue? What does this look like in practice? See how John Woods, author of *Good, Bad, No Dad?* and experienced in pastoral ministry and in training preachers, addresses these questions in

Preaching with fatherlessness in the rear-view mirror
and
Applying the principles: Sermon on Luke 11:1–13 ~ There's More!

in one combined resource
available to download from

https://www.gracepublications.co.uk/good-bad-no-dad-resources

or scan this code to take you straight there

www.gracepublications.co.uk